JENSEN
INTERCEPTOR

JENSEN
INTERCEPTOR

MIKE TAYLOR

CADOGAN BOOKS
LONDON

First published 1983
© Mike Taylor
ISBN 0 946313 60 1

Published by Cadogan Books Limited,
15 Pont Street, London SW1.

Design and Phototypesetting by Logos Design & Advertising,
Datchet, Berkshire.
Printed and bound in Great Britain by
Butler & Tanner Limited, Frome

Dedication
To John and Maria

CONTENTS

INTRODUCTION

I first came into contact with the Jensen and the Jensen Owners' Club in 1976 when I began researching a book on the Sunbeam Tiger sports car. I was told that the person to get in touch with if I wanted information and photographs was John Pellowe. What I did not realise at the time was that my first 'phone call would not only open up a long-standing friendship with John and Maria Pellowe, but would lay the foundations to my introduction to the Jensen Club, its members and their cars. Producing this book on the Interceptor has only served to strengthen the contacts I have made.

Of all Jensen's models, the Interceptor was the one which was made in the greatest numbers. However, among the Company's hierarchy it was also considered the most controversial, and I hope that the reader will feel that I have presented the facts in a fashion which is both fair and unbiased.

Today, we are standing on the brink of what could possibly be a new Jensen era. Jensen Parts and Service, a company which was formed out of the ashes of the old Jensen Motors Limited, have just put the finishing touches to a brand new car – Interceptor '83 – which will be launched at the 1983 Motorfair.

I offer this book as a tribute to their faith in the *marque*.

Mike Taylor
Tunbridge Wells

ACKNOWLEDGEMENTS

When attempting to write a book such as this, it is inevitable that one calls upon a degree of background information which has been gathered over a number of years from many different people and sources. I would therefore like to take this opportunity to thank all those with whom I have come into contact when 'talking Jensen'. Particularly, I would like to thank: Peter Adams, Eileen Beattie, Janet and Clive Fleay, Anthony Good, Hal Kendall, Norman Long, Mike Lotwis, Eric Neale, Ian Orford, John Pellowe, Peter Sbardella, Brian Spicer, Alf Vickers, William Towns, Peter Williams.

Mike Taylor
Tunbridge Wells

P66 – AND ALL THAT

In one of their original pre-war advertisements, Jensen declared that 'Jensens are for Gentlemen'. Today, the Interceptor is a prestige motor car which is enjoyed by a cross section of enthusiasts who appreciate its stylish looks, its effortless performance, and its extravagant refinement: hallmarks of Jensen Motors Limited, established in 1934 by the Jensen brothers, Richard and Alan. Great innovators, they constantly looked ahead in a search for new methods and materials and, with the financial support from their sub-contract work, were able to experiment with, among other things, glass fibre.

In the immediate post-war period Jensen were in the process of developing a new luxury saloon called the PW. Looking somewhat similar to the Austin Sheerline, it was intended that the PW would be powered by the Nash Straight 8 engine but, at the time, the British Government were imposing limitations on imports and would not give permission for these American engines to be brought into the country. As there were only a handful of pre-war engines in stock at Jensen's West Bromwich headquarters, Richard Jensen began negotiations with Henry Meadows for the use of the Meadows Straight as an alternative. Unfortunately, the Meadows proved no substitute for the Nash as it was less powerful and unable to give the PW the performance Richard Jensen demanded. The solution was to approach the Austin Motor Corporation at Longbridge for the supply of their 4 litre 6 cylinder engines. From then on the relationship between Jensen and the Austin Motor Corporation flourished and Jensen found themselves under contract to Austin for the construction of A40 'pick-ups' which were based on the Austin Devon chassis and running gear.

'The Special', the first car built by the Jensen brothers, Richard and Alan, which was based on an Austin Seven chassis.

Jensen Motors Limited factory on Kelvin Way, West Bromwich in the mid 50s. A JNSN lorry is just emerging from the first building.

An active and important aspect of Jensen's business was their commercial vehicle operations looked after by Alan Jensen. This is the popular Jen Tug.

Another type of JNSN vehicle was used for coaches. This chassis was specially developed by Jensen to keep kerb weight to a minimum.

But Richard Jensen was not satisfied with the PW. It simply did not match up to his idea of a long distance tourer and, above all, he was dissatisfied with its shape. So he asked his Chief Engineer, the talented Eric Neale, to prepare some suitable designs for a replacement. (Neale had years of experience in the motor industry with Singer, Daimler and Austin after starting his career at Muliners Limited in 1927.) At the time, Eric Neale remarked to Richard Jensen that he found it difficult to understand why Austin had no small sports tourer in their post-war range.

In mid 1949, Richard – armed with Neale's new styling proposals – went to Longbridge to meet the Austin Board to discuss his plans. The foundation of the new car was to be an Austin chassis modified to take Austin's 4 litre engine together with many Austin components in the running gear. Neale's proposed styling showed a close coupled coupé with a long bonnet and rounded snout: a sleek and appealing design for its day.

However, when Richard Jensen returned to West Bromwich the look on his face must have been less than encouraging for it prompted Eric Neale to ask whether his request had been turned down. 'Oh no,' was the reply, 'we have the engines, but they also want us to design and build a suitable sports model for fitting on the A40 chassis and running gear.'

Clearly, Neale's earlier comment on the lack of a sports model in Austin's range had been noted, but the worry uppermost in Richard Jensen's mind was whether his small Development Department would have the space and the manpower to undertake both projects. As Eric Neale now says 'It turned out to mean a lot of work, but it was a successful cliff-hanger for both cars were finished on time: the Jensen for the Earl's Court Show in October, and the A40 sports body for Austin's approval.'

Somehow, the similarity in appearance between the A40 Sports and the new Jensen coupé was of no concern to the men at Longbridge for Austin immediately contracted Jensen to put the A40 Sports into production, a total of some 3,500 cars being made,

The PW saloon, Jensen's first post war vehicle. Its appearance was very similar to the Austin Sheerline of the day, particularly at the front.

Jensen's pre-war cars were often soft top tourers, so it was natural that they should offer the PW with a drophead. (courtesy of J.O.C.)

The London Motor Show with the Jensen Motors stand clearly visible on the right hand side displaying the Interceptor. (courtesy of Ian Orford)

A close-up of the Jensen stand at the 1954 London Motor Show showing the early Interceptor in the foreground and newly launched 541 behind. (courtesy of Ian Orford)

while Jensen's own new coupé – called the Interceptor – was well received and Jensen found themselves in the exclusive market of the high performance tourer.

The Interceptor used a lengthened A70 chassis with the centre portion of the cruciform lowered to reduce the car's overall height. With the 6 cylinder Austin engine and four speed gearbox, maximum speed was timed at 102 mph, while acceleration from 0-60 mph took 13.1 seconds. A hardtop version was also offered.

By the early 1950s, the Jensens' business was running smoothly. They had a profitable commercial vehicle operation looked after by Alan Jensen, while Richard, the younger brother, was the company's Managing Director and, as the car enthusiast, developed and produced the private cars. The Interceptor had gained a good reputation and Jensen were determined that their next model would be even better.

The 541 was born in February 1953. Like its predecessor it was powered by Austin's 4 litre engine and gearbox, but it embraced all that was new in European G.T. styling. Since it featured a glass fibre body a special peripheral chassis had been designed for it which utilised large diameter tubes and a box section centre structure to give it strength. To determine the position of the seats and rear axle a seating buck had been used. The front wheel centre line was made as far forward as possible to off-set the weight of the engine and gearbox to produce a 50/50 weight distribution when the car was loaded. Like the Interceptor, the 541 used mainly Austin A70 suspension and steering components.

Surprisingly, it seems that the actual styling for the 541 had not been finalised until some time after work on the chassis and drive train had begun. Eric Neale had produced some design proposals from which the eventual 541 shape had been developed. The body itself was made from three separate glass fibre mouldings: the bonnet with special strengthening mouldings to give it extra support, the roof moulding (including the pillars) and the scuttle, and the rear section from the doors back. Rather than make up special

The Interceptor in hard top form. This car was powered by a six cylinder Austin engine giving the car a maximum speed of 102 mph. (courtesy of Ian Orford)

A front view of the Interceptor. A smaller version of this car was built under contract to Austin and was known as the A40 Sports.(courtesy of Ian Orford)

The interior of the Interceptor showing its veneer dashboard and leather trim.

frames for the doors, these were made from alloy. An unusual design feature of the 541 was a swivelling flap covering the air intake to the radiator which could be operated by the driver from inside the car.

The first prototype 541 had been panelled in alloy and, still unfinished, went on display at the Earl's Court Show in 1953. It attracted favourable comments and many prospective customers. When the Show was over and the car back at the factory the final modifications were made to the exhaust system and steering, and arrangements were made to make the body moulds before production could begin in earnest.

To give the car reasonable performance the 541 was fitted with the 4 litre 6 cylinder Austin engine but with a special manifold to accommodate triple SU carburettors. In this state of tune, and with an increased compression ratio, the engine developed 125 bhp and the 541 had a maximum speed of 117 mph.

While the 541 had been the first four-seater production car to utilise a glass fibre body, the 541 de luxe, which was announced in October 1956, was the first production car to be fitted with disc brakes on all four wheels. This was followed 12 months later by the 541R which had closer ratios with the Laycock overdrive unit as standard equipment. Early 541Rs had the 140 bhp twin carburettor engine, while later cars were fitted with the same engine but with triple carburettors.

In October 1960 the 541R was replaced by the 541S. Major structural alterations had been made which included increasing the width between the chassis rails and a re-arranged suspension to give a wider track front and back. These changes increased both interior legroom and rear headroom. Also the interior was considerably altered, being better equipped, even to the fitment of seat belts – the first car on the British market to feature them. However, the car retained the Austin engine in triple carburettor form but linked to a Rolls-Royce-made four-speed automatic transmission which drove a Power-Lok limited slip differential. The car came complete with radio, first aid kit, fire extinguisher and twin spot lamps. Although some critics found its styling a little fussy, the 541S represented a continued effort on Jensen's part to keep abreast of the current trends

A proud Eric Neale stands with the car he styled. This particular car is Ron Smith's award winning 541 R.

The prototype 541 which featured an alloy body. Production cars would use glass fibre bodies based on a specially designed peripheral chassis. (courtesy of J.O.C.)

in high performance Grand Tourers.

The 541 was superseded by the C-V8 in 1962. The chassis was a ladder frame type – designed by Richard Jensen – which used large diameter parallel tubes. The suspension remained similar to that used on the 541, but with softer springs and it had rack and pinion steering. As for the body styling, the theme of the 541 Series had been carried over to the C-V8 but incorporated a reshaped boot, a design originally made by Richard Jensen some years earlier, while the twin headlamp treatment was the result of styling proposals by Eric Neale.

But the major difference between the 541 and the C-V8 was that Jensen had decided to drop the ageing Austin engine in favour of an even bigger, and far more powerful, Chrysler V8 unit, the intention being to considerably uprate the car's performance while making it much more relaxing to drive by offering automatic transmission. The 5.9 litre Chrysler engine, which produced 305 bhp, gave the car a maximum speed of 132 mph and acceleration from 0- 60 mph in 8.4 seconds. This drove through the famous Torqueflite automatic transmission, although manual transmission could be specified. Jensen notched up another 'first' with the C-V8, too, for it was the first production car in Britain to be offered with an alternator in place of the dynamo. The result of all this was a car with a somewhat contentious design, but outstanding performance, which made its debut at the 1962 Earl's Court Motor Show.

The following year the C-V8 received a few minor alterations which included the addition of Armstrong Selectaride adjustable dampers. Later, the 5.9 litre engine was superseded by the more powerful 6.2 litre version which developed 330 bhp at 4,800 rpm. Then, in July 1965, the Mk III C-V8 appeared. This featured dual-circuit braking, a heated rear window and a slightly deeper windscreen. There was less brightwork around the front lights, which subtly altered its appearance. A handful of C-V8 convertibles were made as well.

The production 541. It was the first 100 mph plus saloon to be built using glass fibre. Maximum speed was 112 mph and the standing ¼ mile was timed at 18 secs. (courtesy of J.O.C.)

The engine compartment of Ron Smith's late model 541 R. Early models had twin carburettors mounted on the right while subsequent 541 Rs had their triple carbs mounted on the left.

Another view of Ron Smith's 541 R engine bay. Of 3,993 ccs, by 1960 the unit was heavy and inefficient when compared to other engines.

A novel feature of the 541 range was this moveable flap which, operated by the drive, controlled the flow of air to the radiator.

The 541 was certainly a graceful looking car. This particular model was once owned by racing driver Gerry Marshall, and is seen here outside the Red Lion pub, Cropredy, Oxon.

Interior of the 541 R. Note the extra instruments and radio added below the dashboard.

In an attempt at giving the occupants more room, Jensen increased the width of the 541 when developing the 541 S. Also the swivelling flap was replaced by a conventional grille. It was the first car on the British market to be equipped with seat belts. (courtesy of Ian Orford)

A rear view of the prototype 541 S. Passengers gained more head room from the re-designed body. The car came complete with twin spot lamps, fire extinguisher, first aid kit and radio. (courtesy of Ian Orford)

A front view of the 541 S showing the twin spot lamps which were standard equipment. Behind the grille is a radiator blind which replaced the swivelling flap of the 541 R.

Without doubt, the C-V8 was a car of strong contrasts. Everyone agreed that the car's standard of performance and trim were extremely high, but most found the car's looks bulbous and gross at a time when styles from Italy were sleek and refined. During this period, C-V8 production was a mere two or three cars per week – Jensen's major cash flow coming from their thriving sub-contract work which, in addition to manufacturing the Austin Healey, now included a new contract recently signed with The Rootes Group for the development and construction of the Ford V8-engined Sunbeam Alpine, the Tiger.

In 1964/65 Richard Jensen and Eric Neale set about designing a soft-top tourer, code-named P66 or Project 66. The car was a convertible with lines very characteristic of the models which emerged from the European styling houses during the 1950s, with smooth curves and an aggressive-looking snout. It was fashioned from aluminium and utilised the C-V8 front suspension with a de Dion tube at the rear located by semi elliptic leaf springs. There was a choice of power unit, either the 4.5 litre or 6.3 Chrysler V8 unit. The car went on display at the 1965 London Motor Show.

Significantly, the general trend in the high performance market at this time was towards closed coupés, so the new Jensen was in conflict with its competitors. And the fact that the P66 was some £1,285 cheaper than the C-V8 was to create considerable comment both inside and outside Jensen. Eric Neale explained, 'The P66 was never intended as a replacement for the C-V8. In fact, we had no plans for a C-V8 successor at that time. It was intended as a sports car mainly for the American market which, had it gone into production, would have taken over from the Austin Healey when it was eventually withdrawn. There would have been no difficulties over safety or emission control regulations and the planned production rate was 25-30 units per week. The Americans

This particular 541 S was once owned by Donald Healey and was fitted with a 327 cu. in. Chrysler V8 engine.

were very sad that it never reached production.' The sales brochure said: 'Designed to fill a gap in the motoring market, the Jensen Interceptor (P66) is a high speed touring car with a sporting feel'. Clearly, if ever a car was misinterpreted, the P66 must be it, for few people saw its potential.

A combination of ill-health and the need for greater financial support had forced the Jensen brothers into putting the business into the hands of a holding company (Norcros) in June 1959. They, in turn, had put their own Managing Director, Michael Day, a former employee of British Aviation Services. But Day remained a mere 12 months and was replaced by Brian Owen.

In 1960, Kevin Beattie joined the company. Beattie had begun his career in the motor industry as a pupil at Rootes and had emerged as a very talented and capable engineer. His criticism of the C-V8 was that it was a styling disaster. Nevertheless, he felt that the P66 was not a car capable of creating good sales and maintaining the company's image in the market of Grand Touring cars. He began to campaign strongly for an all-new, Italian-styled car which he saw as the only solution to the problem.

Not surprisingly, the Jensens were appalled by this idea. They favoured British designs and were proud of their own ability to design, develop, and make cars in-house. Since Kevin Beattie's job was centred around chassis development, the fact that he was making his feelings felt over the future of the P66 created strong criticism. But despite the formidable opposition of the Jensen brothers to Beattie's suggestions, he had a powerful ally in Brian Owen. And Beattie's views were further shared by John Sheffield, who was Managing Director of Norcros.

The 541 S was replaced by the C-V8 in 1962 and was powered by a Chrylsler V8 engine which improved its performance dramatically. Maximum speed was well over 130 mph. (courtesy of Ian Orford)

The engine bay of the C-V8. This particular C-V8 is the award winning car owned by Dave Horton. (courtesy of J.O.C.)

Major engineering work being carried out on a C-V8 showing the assembly of the extremely strong rear boot area which was formed from sheet steel which was welded to the chassis beneath. (courtesy of Birmingham Evening Mail)

Engineers working on the C-V8 test rig. Well known for its longevity these Chrysler engines give trouble-free motoring clocking up very high mileages. (courtesy of Birmingham Evening Mail)

The Jensen Motors Board as it comprised in late 1963. Richard and Alan Jensen are fourth and fifth from left.

The P66 with its 50s-like appearance. This car was to have been an addition to the Jensen range, selling mainly in America. Engine options were to be either the 4.4 or the 6.3 litre Chrysler V8 units.
(courtesy of Ian Orford)

Interior of the P66 taken on display at the 1965 London Motor Show. The four-wheel-drive C-V8 is in the background.

A side view, reproduced from the company's brochure, of the P66. Notice the wheelarch treatment and compare it to the picture below. (courtesy of J.O.C.)

Jensen's stand at the 1965 Motor Show strongly indicated the company's optimism for the future: neither car on display, the P66 or the four-wheel-drive C-V8, had reached production. (courtesy of Ian Orford)

After designing a soft top version, Eric Neale styled this fixed hard top P66, the regular lines of the roof and the different wheel arch treatment improving the car considerably. (courtesy of Ian Orford)

A close-up of the frontal treatment of the hard top P66 showing the elimination of the small grilles beside the headlamps. In all, two P66s were made as roadgoing prototypes, one in white, the second in metallic green.
(courtesy of Ian Orford)

Chapter Two

ACHIEVING THE IMPOSSIBLE

The argument Kevin Beattie used so convincingly was that, although the C-V8 had proved itself as having oustanding performance and road manners – the motoring magazines had all said as much – the car's main weakness was its contentious shape. What was needed, he argued, was a new G.T. model with strengths which lay in the areas where the C-V8 was weak. Jensen were not – and never had been – makers of thoroughbred motor cars, but they were makers of exclusive high quality G.T.s and, like haute couture, above all they had to look right.

Beattie finally won his case and went to Italy for a tour of the styling houses. His intention was to secure a design which would fit onto the existing C-V8 chassis and drive train, retaining the C-V8's wheelbase and track. He asked Touring, Ghia and Vignale to submit designs based on these requirements. Unfortunately, Ghia's fee was unacceptable as Beattie was working within a limited budget. Those designs presented by Vignale were considered a little too conventional. However, Beattie was impressed by Touring's design, which was finally decided upon for the car which would replace the C-V8.

But Touring were unable to take the project any further, so Jensen bought the plans outright, removed all traces of Touring's authorship, and took them along to the Vignale studios where, in early 1966, a contract was signed to get the new car into production –

Kevin Beattie, the driving force behind the decision to scrap the P66 in favour of an Italian styled car, the Interceptor, which was launched in 1966.

Richard Jensen, known throughout the company as 'Mr Richard'. He and brother Alan, were outraged at the idea of going to Italy for a styling proposal but, in the end they were over-ruled.

giving the team just ten months to get the car to the Earl's Court Motor Show that year. This was a formidable task by any standards, but made all the more difficult because of the distance between Milan and West Bromwich.

However, the job of getting the new car into production was made easier because it would use the chassis of the C-V8 almost intact, leaving only the body and interior to be concentrated upon. As soon as the deal was signed a C-V8 was sent to Italy where the fibre glass body was removed and within three months Vignale had a new body finished, awaiting Jensen's approval. Then, only a month after that, Kevin Beattie was back in Milan to test drive the first prototype.

This was a particularly difficult time for Kevin Beattie. Not only did he have to face the continuing misgivings of the Jensen brothers, he also had to co-ordinate the production of the new car. As he later admitted, he had had his hands full enough without the complication of internal politics.

That Kevin Beatie was able to achieve the near impossible can perhaps be attributed to two factors: that he alone was the car's Development *and* Production Engineer, and that, in March 1966, he brought in a long-time friend, Richard Graves, to help with sales promotion. Graves, who had left Rolls-Royce to join Jensen, brought with him enthusiasm and a whole new approach to marketing. As public relations expert Tony Good said recently' 'I think the Jensen brothers never looked over their shoulders at anyone and would have been surprised to be compared to a company such as Aston Martin. Also, I think they were totally misread. I remember saying to Richard Jensen on one occasion, 'You must be a very proud man because, to the best of my knowledge, you are the only motor manufacturer who has his own name on the front of his car', to which he replied 'Well you are absolutely wrong, because whenever anyone comes to look at my cars I always want to say, "Don't buy this one, wait until next year when we will have something much better".'

Unfortunately, this almost naive enthusiasm had tended to overshadow the hard facts of making and selling motor cars. As soon as Graves arrived he was confronted by the difficult task of selling the remaining C-V8s, before the arrival of the new car, at a time when most Jensen dealers were aware that the C-V8's replacement was being launched at the Earl's Court Show.

When it was finally shown on the Jensen stand in October 1966 the car – called 'Interceptor' – was an outstanding success. The car was built of steel whereas the 541 and the C-V8 had both been constructed in fibre glass. Why? The answer was simply that, as Jensen had gone to Vignale for the Interceptor bodies, and since Vignale always worked in metal, there was no choice. However, there are probably some Interceptor owners who now wish that their cars had been made from glass fibre!

Clearly, it was the superb lines of the Interceptor which drew such admiring glances from those who saw the car during those days at Earl's Court. The aggressively-shaped nose and slightly curved bonnet would stand the test of time, while the raked windscreen gave the car a very sleek appearance when viewed from the side. Only the downsweep of the waist towards the rear threatened to date the car.

Inside the car Jensen had maintained their tradition of hand-built cars of quality, and the new Interceptor was no exception. Leather trim and deep pile Wilton carpet were used throughout. The dashboard had two hooded dials ahead of the driver and supplementary instruments and switches placed on a centre console. Of certain appeal to prospective buyers were its cavernous 16 cu.ft. boot (ideal for stowing all those suitcases for long Continental journeys) and its superlative seating designed to keep driver and passengers comfortable over those long miles.

The re-bodied C-V8 at Vignale's factory before being brought back to England. The wooden form in the foreground left, was used to make the body panels. (courtesy of Ian Orford)

Inspecting the first Interceptor prototype. Vignale and his team had removed the C-V8 body and produced the sleek replacement in just four months. (courtesy of Ian Orford)

Kevin Beattie, obviously taking advantage of the Italian weather, while enjoying a break from driving the new Jensen. (courtesy of Ian Orford)

Another view inside Vignale's factory showing the wooden shapes from which the tin smiths and panel beaters produced the steel bodyshell. (courtesy of Ian Orford)

Taking on petrol before the trip home. Notice the change in the weather. (courtesy of Ian Orford)

Kevin getting to grips with the Interceptor. The rev counter showing 3,400 rpm – about 88 mph – the car well within its capabilities. (courtesy of Ian Orford)

The Vignale built prototype is carefully reversed off the British United aircraft. The Touring Superleggera styling was certainly different to the Jensen styled C-V8. (courtesy of Ian Orford)

The interior of a Mk 1 Interceptor. Jensen had already established a reputation for high quality craftsmanship and the Interceptor was to carry on in this tradition. (courtesy of Ian Orford)

A detail shot of a Mk 1 Interceptor headlight and bumper arrangement. On this model, the side light and indicator are mounted above the bumper. (courtesy of Ian Orford)

Jack Nicklaus with his Mk 1 Interceptor. Jensens became very popular with celebrities over the years. Among those who drove Interceptors were the novelist Harold Robbins and comedy team, Mike and Bernie Winters.

Get rich slow.

There are still some under-privileged areas in England where a man can't buy a Jensen car.

To put that right, we're appointing four new Jensen distributors to cover the following areas:

1. Hampshire and Dorset.
2. Gloucestershire, Wiltshire, Somerset, Devon and Cornwall.
3. Oxfordshire and Berkshire.
4. Bedfordshire, Hertfordshire and Essex.

We must admit that we don't make many cars (less than 20 a week). So you're not going to make a fortune overnight. But when you do sell one, your bank manager will certainly know about it.

If you're interested in selling and servicing Jensens, write to our Marketing Director, R. A. Graves. The address is Jensen Motors Ltd, Kelvin Way, West Bromwich.

To start with, all we need to know is the location of your showroom, your current franchises and the name of your bank.

Do it soon. We'd hate someone else to get the business.

A Mk 1 Interceptor used in an advertisement to encourage motor traders to become dealers for Jensen cars. However, they do admit to making less that twenty cars per week. (courtesy of Ian Orford)

Another celebrity taking delivery of his Jensen, this time a Mk 1 FF, is Jazz musician Ginger Baker.

Designer Jon Bannenberg produced this Director version of the Interceptor which gave the executive in a hurry a complete office on wheels. It included a typewriter, dictation machine, filing system, Air-Call radio and television. (courtesy of Ian Orford)

Pat Follet (with glasses) and Carl Duerr, on the occasion in August 1969, when Jensen produced their 1000th Interceptor. Follett, Managing Director of Charles Follett Ltd., was presented with a silver plaque

Making the sturdy chassis unit which formed the foundation of the Interceptor body. The rear inner wheel arch sections can be clearly seen.

The chassis unit removed from its jig with the floor pans and front suspension mounting in position.

The almost completed chassis on its trolley before being taken to the body making jig. The stays between the bulkhead and chassis help give the structure additional strength.

The body/chassis unit being dipped in the primer tank supervised by Works Manager, Bill Silvester. After dipping, approximately 4 gallons remained on the unit covering it completely. (courtesy of Ian Orford)

The body assembly lines with the Interceptor bodyshells on their trollies being moved along the assembly track.

An early FF bodyshell being tested on the seat belt testing machine. The Jensen 541 S was the first British car to feature seat belts as standard equipment. (courtesy of Ian Orford)

Jensen always prided themselves in a reputation for high quality craftsmanship.
The front seats taking shape

An Interceptor Mk 11 undergoing final preparation before its first road test to establish whether there are any faults

The Motor Show over, the Interceptor production line got under way but it soon became clear that it was uneconomic to continue to import Vignale-built bodies from Italy. So Beattie arranged with Vignale to transfer the body tooling to West Bromwich where Jensen's own workforce would take over the job. Initially, however, this changeover created considerable practical difficulties with the tooling because of Vignale's particular method of body construction, based partly on their experience of working with prototype bodies.

The foundation of the Interceptor consisted of twin 4-inch diameter chassis tubes running between the wheelbase. On to this were welded the front and back cross-members, which were used as the suspension mounting points. Then, to finish the chassis assembly, sheet metal was welded on to form the front and rear bulkhead, floor pan and boot floor. The entire operation took some 44 hours to complete. This structure was then wheeled over to the body assembly area where the inner body panels and wheelarch sections were added before the outer body sections were fitted. After this, the body/chassis unit was cleaned in de-greasing acid and dipped in primer before being sprayed. Finally came the installation of the drive train and the trimming, which took some twelve days to complete.

All Interceptors underwent two road tests. First, a short duration run to assess any obvious faults (which would then be rectified on the car's return to the factory), and then a second, longer 120-miles test to ensure that all was right for the car to leave the factory.

Enthusiasm for the Interceptor ran high among the workforce and the future looked promising. Not since the days of the 541s of the 1950s did Jensen have a product of their own of which they could be so justly proud.

Three years after the launch of the Vignale Interceptor Jensen introduced the Mk II. Attention had been paid to improving the car's ventilation, and air conditioning was available as an optional extra. The front seats had been re-designed to further improve their comfort, a 20-gallon petrol tank fitted to give the car a longer range, and radial-ply tyres replaced the original cross-plys. Underneath, the dampers were changed to a non-adjustable type and modifications made to the front and rear suspension to improve the car's handling qualities. Jensen may have been unhappy with the design of the Mk I's facia, because in the Mk II it had been extensively modified with a better designed dashboard with more up-to-date rocker switches.

By the late 1960s, the Interceptor had established a sound market with the car attracting customers who previously had never bought Jensens. In particular, the Interceptor was being bought by company men. It had suddenly become *the* car for the successful executive to own. And to this end, Jon Bannenberg (who had been responsible for design work on the QE2) was commissioned to re-style the interior for a lavish 'Director' version of the Interceptor. In addition to the usual leather interior, there was an overnight bag and attaché case in matching trim, a dictating machine, a typewriter, a place for filing correspondence, and even a television. As if that was not enough, a food and drinks cabinet, a shaving kit, and an Air Call radio telephone were also part of the specification.

In October 1971 Jensen launched their Mk III Interceptor. This model featured 6½-inch alloy road wheels, with ventilated disc brakes on all wheels. At the same time, Jensen also announced the introduction of the SP (standing for 'Six Pack', meaning six chokes from three dual barrel carburettors) which marked the beginning of Jensen's use of the even larger 7.2 litre Chrysler engine. In this form the unit produced some 50 bhp more than the standard 7.2 litre engine which was used in the Mk III from 1973 onwards. Without doubt, the SP was a handsomely equipped car with all the optional equipment of the MK III car as standard fitments, together with a radio/tape player. Performance, as might be expected, was impressive, although it did not match that of, say, the Aston Martin DBS V8 or the Ferrari Daytona.

The finsihing touches being put to the leather covered rear seat.

The MP for Birmingham admiring an Interceptor Mk 11 on the Jensen stand at the 1970 Motor Show. Next to him is PR executive, Tony Good, with Sales Director, Richard Graves on the right.

A front view of an Interceptor Mk 11 showing the arrangement of the side lights and bumper, which has been moved up improving the looks of the Mk11 cars considerably. (courtesy of J.O.C.)

An under bonnet shot of a Mk 11 Interceptor with the air conditioning unit in front of the giant air cleaner clearly visible. Note the Jensen name on the cam cover. (courtesy of Ian Orford)

A Mk 111 Interceptor showing the alloy road wheels which were also used on the SP. Early cars still retained the 6.3 litre engine but in 1973 they were changed to the 'clean' 7.2 unit.

...the Jensen experience

Only now and again in life do members of our affluent society enjoy the thrill of owning something special—something superior to other products—something peculiarly satisfying to the senses. The Jensen Interceptor III is such an object. Its most important attribute is undoubtedly the fine British workmanship, highlighted by the hand-sewn leather interior. There is an aromatic quality about genuine leather that is lost with use of modern plastics.

The Jensen automobile is not only marketed internationally, it is truly an international product, and represents the very best from two other countries besides Great Britain. It owes its styling to Vignale of Italy, and its superb power train to the Chrysler Corporation. Suspension, steering, and brakes are all British, and are responsible for a medium-firm ride, and road-holding and handling that are difficult to criticize. It is a sturdy vehicle, weighing in excess of 4,000z, which helps give the owner a feeling of security and stability under any conditions of road or weather. Driver comfort is unequalled.

Americans, particularly, spend a lot of time in their automobiles, and to some people it is merely a chore. To owners of a Jensen, however, it becomes something to look forward to. Most Jensen owners have a great feeling of contentment, even excitement, every morning when they start their cars. To some it is a nostalgic feeling because it takes them back to the enjoyment they experienced when they had their first car.

The Jensen is not a passenger car—it certainly isn't a race-car—nor even a true sports car. However it will carry four passengers,

with reasonable comfort, has the quality and finish equal to any car in the world, and will do almost all the things a sports car will do, with smoothness, quietness, and a minimum of effort on the part of the vehicle or the driver. It comes equipped with all the modern conveniences, such as air-conditioning, electric windows, 8-track stereo, and other interesting and unique features.

Our factory is located in West Bromwich, England, but we have built a parts and service network in the United States that stands ready to guarantee you driving pleasure.

If you are a car enthusiast you will love the Jensen. If you're not, the Jensen car will most certainly make you one.

KJELL H. QVALE
Manufacturer

JENSEN MOTORS INC.

A typical advertisement used by Jensen in America after Kjell Qvale's takeover in 1970. Qvale is sitting on the bonnet in the lower picture. (courtesy of Ian Orford)

An Australian customer taking delivery of his Jensen. (courtesy of Ian Orford)

The launch of the Jensen SP at the 1971 London Motor Show. The car was intended to replace the FF as Jensen's flagship of their range. By this time the FF's costly and time-consuming manufacturing process was not considered viable.

The SP featured all the Interceptor's optional extras as standard equipment. With its 'Six Pack' engine, maximum speed was rated at 145 mph.

The louvered bonnet of the SP was not just for show. Like the grille in the rear wing panel, it helped reduce under bonnet temperatures by allowing the hot air to escape.

In 1973 Jensen's stocks of the Six Pack engine were exhausted and the SP model was dropped from the range. By this time, Chrysler, who were desperately trying to keep their engines within the stringent U.S. emission control regulations, had been unable to do so with the Six Pack and so it had been withdrawn. However, the extra equipment of the SP model was incorporated into the latest MK III Interceptor – the J Series – which was fitted with the 'clean' 7.2 litre engine and remained in production until 1976. One final modification worthy of mention which was made to the J Series during its life was the availability of a walnut dashboard, which further enhanced the standard of interior trim.

Remarkably, over the ten years that the Interceptor was in production (despite the changes made to its mechanical and trim specifications) the car's acceleration, maximum speed and weight changed insignificantly. The earliest car weighed 33 cwt and sprinted to 60 mph in 7.3 seconds, while the Mk II did the same speed in just over a second less. Maximum speeds varied between 133 mph for the Mk I and 137 for the MK II. In Mk III form, with the larger 7.2 litre power unit, acceleration from 0-60 mph was 7.7 seconds, while maximum speed was 129 mph.

The front suspension of Peter Sbardella's SP. The ventilated disc brakes were fitted to cope with the car's high performance capabilities.

The shape of the Interceptor saloon was not changed in its 10 year life and towards the end it was beginning to look a little dated. See here how the rear lines of the car give it a squat appearance.

A front view of an early Mk 111 car showing how the design of the bumper was changed yet again. Compare the grille of this car to that fitted to the Interceptor Coupé.

Access to the 16 cu ft boot space was via the large rear screen which was released from inside the car and lifted up. The only criticism is lifting heavy suitcases over the high back panel.

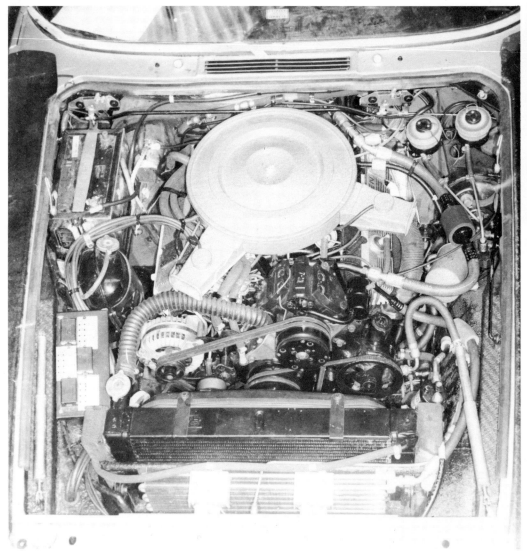

As the Interceptor was modified to conform with emission regulations and boasted more equipment as standard, so its engine bay became more cluttered and complex. (courtesy of Ian Orford)

The Interceptor 'J' Series was introduced in January 1973 when Jensen began fitting the J type 7.2 litre engine. This version was denoted by a figure 'J' on the rear flanks of the car.

The interior of the Mk 111 Interceptor: hide seating and Wilton carpeting setting off the car to good effect. Many Interceptors were bought by company directors who had never before bought Jensens.

A shot of the rear suspension of a Mk 111 Interceptor showing the leaf spring encased in a leather cover and the ventilated disc brake. (courtesy of J.O.C.)

A close-up of the alloy road wheel as fitted to the SP and Interceptor Mk 111. 6½JK x 15, these allowed for plenty of rubber to be in contact with the road to transmit all that power.

A side view of the 'J' Series Interceptor. As Jensen's aggressive marketing became more effective Jensens were seen in America, South Africa, Australia and Japan.

Chapter Three

F, FF AND FFF

Harry Ferguson was a wealthy tractor manufacturer who had a particular interest in vehicle safety. During a meeting with veteran racing ace, Freddie Dixon, the possibility was discussed of making a car with four-wheel-drive. Someone else who was interested in the project was racing enthusiast Tony Rolt, and together the three men began experiments with a prototype vehicle powered by a 1.5 litre ERA engine. This car not only had four-wheel-drive, but four-wheel-steering, too, the latter being achieved by turning the axles rather than turning the wheels, the front and back being locked together in a push-pull arrangement.

In the event the scheme was a failure, although the three men remained committed to the project. A successful lawsuit against Henry Ford then provided Ferguson with ample funds to establish Harry Ferguson Research (which he set up in 1950) and Dixon and Rolt joined the company as Directors. However, the real breakthrough came when Claude Hill (well known in Aston Martin circles as a chassis and engine designer) joined the group and developed a self-locking differential. This divided the torque between the front and rear axles thereby improving handling.

The original Jensen FF which was based on a C-V8 body. Painted red, it was seen on display at the 1965 London Motor Show but with the introduction of the Touring designed Interceptor, the car was never put into production. (courtesy of Ian Orford)

The team and their C-V8 taking part in the Commanders Cup at Snetterton in 1965. It was here that Brian Spicer, who became Jensen's Chief Development Engineer (first from left in fig. B) came into contact with Kevin Beattie (holding umbrella) (courtesy of Ian Orford)

Like the Mk 1 Interceptor, the early FFs had a low slung front bumper mounted below the side lights. This car has been fitted with radial tyres although radials were not fitted until the introduction of Mk 11 cars.
(courtesy of J.O.C.)

The technically brilliant FF can be distinguished from the standard Interceptor by the extra vent in the rear of the front wing. The car is also 3 inches longer. (courtesy of J.O.C.)

Throughout the 1950s, work went well and the company had a degree of success. Another aspect of their work was the application of the Dunlop Maxaret anti-skid braking system, which furthered the team's advancement towards safer vehicles. One particular project was the Ferguson R5, a four-wheel-drive estate vehicle. Said to be capable of 100 mph, it was powered by Ferguson's own flat four engine which the firm had designed and developed. The plan was for the car to be built by a number of companies, each contributing towards its construction and marketing. One of those companies was Jensen Motors Limited.

But the project was beset with difficulties in attempting to secure agreement among the companies involved. Later an agreement was reached between Ferguson and Jensen whereby the latter company would use the four-wheel-drive Maxaret system in a Jensen vehicle. Although this contract was finalised in 1962, the finished Jensen four-wheel-drive was not seen until the 1965 Motor Show. This delay was due to pressure of work at Jensen in putting the Sunbeam Tiger into production.

In fact, although this first four-wheel-drive Jensen (a modified C-V8 and called the Jensen FF) was exhibited on Jensen's stand – along with the ill-fated P66 – the car was not complete at that stage for it did not even have an engine. Although the bonnet was kept tightly closed at the Show, no one was fooled! Nevertheless, it had been a feat of engineering, for the FF (standing for Ferguson Formula) C-V8 was quite a different vehicle from its conventional brother. To begin with, getting the four-wheel-drive unit in the drive line had meant increasing the length of the car by some four inches, which had been achieved by adding an extra section of body/chassis from the windscreen forwards.

The engine and transmission of the FF were identical to that used in the conventional C-V8, using the Chrysler engine the Torqueflite automatic gearbox but in the case of the FF, off-set to one side. The four-wheel-drive system was located at the rear of the transmission unit and drove the rear wheels through a normal propeller shaft, although the Power-Lok differential of the standard C-V8 had not been incorporated as it was thought to be unnecessary. Drive to the front wheels was taken via another propeller shaft, this time connected to one side of the front of the four-wheel-drive unit, and connected to a Salisbury final drive unit where drive was subsequently taken to the front wheels by universally jointed half shafts.

To accommodate this radical change in transmission arrangement, the chassis and front suspension had been substantially altered from that used on the normal C-V8. To allow for the shafts to connect with the front wheels, dual springs were fitted either side of the shafts, with integral dampers. Power assisted steering was standard equipment.

The whole idea of the Jensen four-wheel-drive layout using Maxaret anti-skid braking was to prevent (a) the car's wheels from skidding (which would normally happen under heavy braking and would be prevented by the Maxaret unit) and (b) the wheels from spinning (which would normally occur on slippery road surfaces and would be taken care of by the four-wheel-drive unit). Simply, drive to the rear wheels was fed via the input shaft to the four-wheel-drive unit and through a master differential and out to the rear propeller shaft. This master differential also drove a Morse Hyvo chain which provided rotation to the front wheels as well as feeding into one side of a control unit. The other feed to the control unit was taken from the input shaft from the engine.

The principle of operation was that in the case of either the front or rear wheels beginning to spin, the control unit would detect whether the speed of rotation of the front output shaft was faster or slower than the rotation speed of the input shaft. Beyond the pre-set limits of over-run – at which the front wheels could over run the rear or vice versa – the control unit would then lock the main differential and reduce the rotation speed of the shaft to the spinning wheels. Should the wheels lock under braking, then the same system would apply and drive would be restored through the main differential. However, in this case the Maxaret unit would control the electrically operated vacuum servo unit in the braking system, momentarily reducing its effectiveness until the skidding wheels regained their grip.

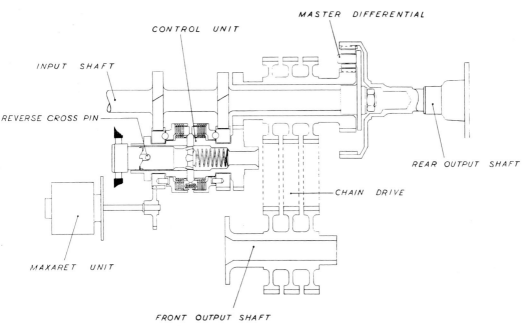

INPUT SHAFT

CONTROL UNIT

MASTER DIFFERENTIAL

REVERSE CROSS PIN

MAXARET UNIT

REAR OUTPUT SHAFT

CHAIN DRIVE

FRONT OUTPUT SHAFT

4-WHEEL DRIVE UNIT (FERGUSON FORMULA)

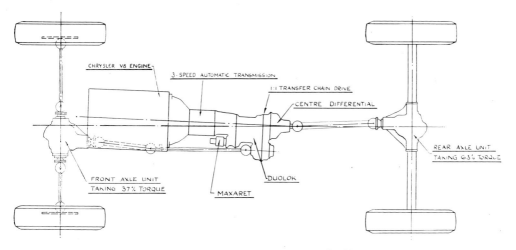

CHRYSLER V8 ENGINE

3-SPEED AUTOMATIC TRANSMISSION

1:1 TRANSFER CHAIN DRIVE

CENTRE DIFFERENTIAL

REAR AXLE UNIT
TAKING 63% TORQUE

FRONT AXLE UNIT
TAKING 37% TORQUE

DUOLOK

MAXARET

TRANSMISSION LAYOUT

Schematic drawings showing the layout of the four-wheel-drive system as fitted to the Jensen. Although the principle of driving all four wheels was well accepted by the press, the Maxaret anti-lock braking was less liked.

A Mk 11 FF. Some road test reports hailed the FF as the 'safest car in the world', and certainly the Mk 11 with its modified suspension, more refined interior and greater power was an improvement over the Mk 1.

When Kevin Beattie decided to begin his crusade to replace the P66 project with an all-new model, a factor which was uppermost in his mind was a four-wheel-drive variant. Development Engineer Brian Spicer explained, 'I was working at Dunlop's braking division as their Chief Development Engineer when we won an order from Ford for braking equipment. At this point, Girling – who normally supplied Ford with their braking – got quite excited and simply bought out my division from Dunlop. They then offered me a job, but Kevin Beattie (whom I had known from previous work with the C-V8) asked me to join him at Jensen.

'When I arrived at Jensen, the red C-V8 FF was just about to be put on the stand at Earl's Court,' continued Spicer. 'I think that Kevin, who was a chassis engineer – and a good chassis engineer – would have liked to have gone for a more futuristic chassis on the Interceptor but, because of the turmoil over the Italian body, there was no way he could have considered changing the chassis as well as the body. So the decision was made to stick with the C-V8 chassis because it was proven: it worked on the C-V8 and there was no reason why it shouldn't work on the new Interceptor. But Kevin wanted to bring in something which was really new and advanced. Then, after Richard Graves had joined us he began pushing for the FF from a sales aspect probably as much as Kevin wanted to do it.'

Getting the ordinary Interceptor into production would have been a sufficient challenge for most men, but Kevin Beattie was determined to have a double attraction on the Jensen stand at the 1966 Motor Show, and he put all his energies into achieving this goal. 'Kevin was a great guy in that he knew precisely where he was going,' commented Brian Spicer. 'He would never raise his voice but if, for example, you were discussing a certain project with him he would probably ask how things were going and then why this or that hadn't been tried. Afterwards, you'd walk out of the meeting and suddenly think, 'I've had my backside kicked', but you'd never know it at the time.'

A front view of a Jensen FF Mk 11. Like the Interceptor Mk 11, the FF benefitted from the altered position of the front bumper.

A test rig specially designed for developing a left hand drive version of the FF which unfortunately never came into production. (courtesy of Ian Orford)

Another view of the FF test rig for developing a left hand drive version. In the event too few sales of right hand drive cars made the project not viable. (courtesy of Ian Orford)

The Jensen Nova. This car was styled by Vignale and was based on an Interceptor chassis shortened by 5 inches.
The stylish body was fashioned from glass fibre. (courtesy of J.O.C.)

Brian Spicer with his car 'Big Bertha', which was the rolling test bed for the chassis and suspension development for what would have been the Interceptor's replacement.

The engine compartment of 'Big Bertha', showing how by, lengthening the chassis by six inches, created space between the bulkhead and transmission.

With such a tight time schedule it was fortunate that Vignale's work force were able to produce the prototypes with such speed. Brian Spicer again: 'I remember talking the FF project over with Kevin when he said, 'Brian, I want you to arrange for the body to be taken off a C-V8 so that we can send it over to Vignale for them to put a prototype body on it,'. To which I said, 'Why aren't we doing it?' Kevin replied, 'Can we do it in eight weeks?' I had to admit that we couldn't.'

It was Brian Spicer's job to co-ordinate all the arrangements for getting the FF through development and into production. Since they were using tried components, many of the difficulties of meeting the completion date were alleviated. 'We had to do some rig testing on wishbones and vertical pins on the front suspension,' recalled Brian, 'but other than that, there were few difficulties with the FF. If there were any troubles at all, it was in the four-wheel-drive unit itself. The original FF unit had never been designed to go into a car like the Interceptor with 300 hp to muscle it along. The Morse chain was already over engineered, so that gave us no trouble. But the little intricacies of the free wheel unit, for example, proved incapable of handling the torque that was produced from the Chrysler engine.' Fortunately, Ferguson's Coventry-based research laboratory was not far from Jensen's West Bromwich headquarters. Tony Rolt, Derek Gardner and Jim Walker formed the basis of the development team, and soon the four-wheel-drive unit was running properly.

'Big Bertha', is also 4 inchest wider than a standard Interceptor and to accommodate the large wheels, big
wheel arches had to be fitted hence the name.

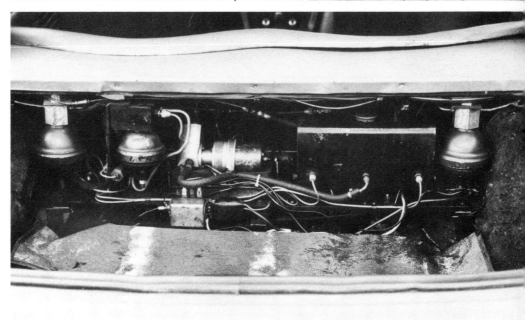

The Girling designed self levelling suspension system developed for the F Type, the Interceptor's replacement.

Like the Interceptor, the FF was extremely well received at the 1966 Motor Show. The hard work and long hours had been worth it, and although the FF never went on to become a big seller, it is thought that the car paid for itself in publicity alone. As Tony Good said later, 'The FF was the car in the showroom window which sold the Interceptor in the basement'. It is unlikely that people bought FFs solely for their incredibly safe handling qualities, but rather because they were highly prestigious motor cars. 'We did talk on many occasions of putting the FF into competitive motor sport,' said Brian Spicer, 'but it was never thought to be viable.'

One vehicle (a spin-off, if you like!) of the FF was the FFF 100, which was a special four-wheel-drive car developed by FF Developments in conjunction with GKN. The intention was to use the vehicle as a rolling test bed for the development of new concepts using the anti-skid braking and four-wheel-drive layout. It was powered by a 7 litre Chyrsler Hemi, tuned to produce over 600 bhp and drove through a Chrysler automatic gearbox. Not surprisingly, the car had outstanding performance and sprinted from 0-100-0 mph in 12.2 seconds in the wet and 11.5 seconds in the dry at the Motor Industry's Research Association's test track at Nuneaton.

Unfortunately, no sooner had Jensen put the FF into production than Jensen's Sales and Production Departments pointed out that, despite its unquestioned publicity value, the car was too costly to make since much of it was peculiar to the FF and the volume of sales could not justify it. Moreover, with part of the manpower tied up in manufacturing FFs this effectively limited the number of Interceptors they could make. What was needed was another flagship, but one which was based on the Interceptor. The result was the SP.

In 1970 a Mk II Interceptor was taken off the production line and modified to take the larger 7.2 litre triple carburettor engine. The purpose of this vehicle was to test the Interceptor with the more powerful engine and finally homologate it for production. When this project was completed the car was then stripped down in readiness for a more ambitious programme which Jensen were just about to begin.

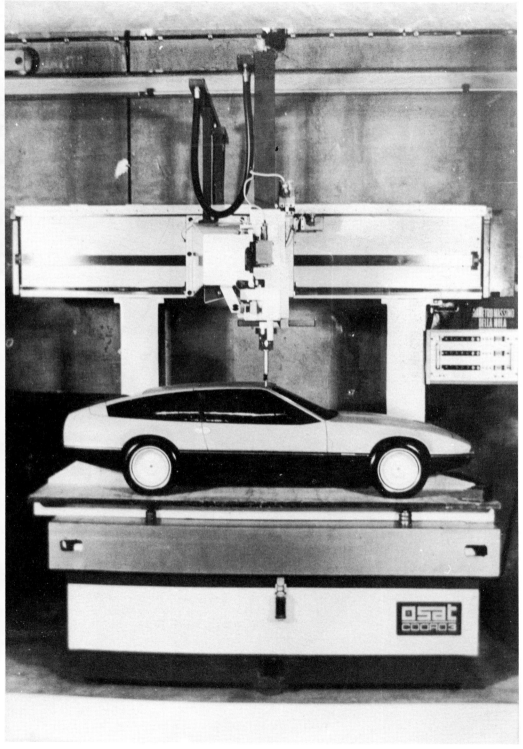

William Towns' scale model of the F Type on the tracing platform at Industor, which transposed the dimensions of the model into working drawings.

The F Type prototype. Notice the curvature of the roof line and the slight rise in the lower edge of the rear window, which gave the car a very contemporary appearance.

At the same time, Kevin Beattie and Kjell Qvale (who had recently taken over the controlling interest in Jensen Motors Limited) were beginning to turn their attentions to a car which would supersede the Interceptor. Although, by this time, Interceptor sales were reasonably strong, they did not want to be in a position of suffering flagging sales (as in the case of the C-V8) before introducing a new model, and several of the world's top automotive stylists were asked to submit proposals: Bertone, Trevor Fiore, Ital Design and William Towns among them. In the event, it was Towns' design which was finally accepted.

This immediately committed the company to a large capital investment programme to develp the car – known at this stage as the F Type – and put it into production. Nevertheless, Beattie was concerned that the company should retain the image that the Interceptor had created. The specification for the F Type combined the latest styling trends with superior aero-dynamics; although it would be powered by the same 7.2 litre Chrysler engine with full Californian emission control equipment. Inside, the car was to have more room for driver and passengers, and of particular importance was that, although the car was to be a two-door, passengers could get into the back without those sitting in the front having to get out of the car. For this reason it had extra large doors. Towns recalls that after a styling colleague had described the roof line of the Lamborghini Espada – which maintained a continuous curvature from the windscreen to the rear of the car – he, too, embraced this theme in his proposal for the F Type, together with another Espada feature, a small glass panel in the transom.

A 0.4 scale model was produced from clay and after being approved by Jensen was sent to Industor in Italy where the design was transposed into full-size technical drawings. The drawings were then sent to Coggilla who produced a full-size plaster replica and, after a few small modifications had been made, Coventry Motor Panels were then contracted to make five prototype bodyshells.

In this view, the glass panel in the transom of the car can be clearly seen. It was intended that the F Type would have stayed in production well into the 1980s, had Jensen remained in business.

Meanwhile, the Mk II Interceptor which had been used in the SP programme was being modified to test the proposed suspension for the F Type. Since the F Type was to be a bigger car all round than the Interceptor, the prototype car was considerably modified to make it into a suitable test bed for developing the new suspension. The body/chassis unit was lengthened by six inches between the front pillar and the front wheel arch, and the track was widened by four inches. With its wide profile tyres and wheel arch extension, the car soon got the nickname 'Big Bertha'.

A great deal of consideration was given to the suspension and chassis design for the F Type, so that not only the car's looks but its ride and handling, too, would represent an improvement on the Interceptor. It was important that the suspension system gave excellent handling, irrespective of load, while not encroaching on interior space. The solution was a de Dion rear suspension supported on low rate leaf springs, Watts linkage and an anti-roll bar assisted by a Girling self-levelling system. The tyres were to be 245 x 15, which were specially designed and made for the project.

Another reason for using these wide tyres was the large internal rim diameter which aided the efficiency of the front brakes while giving a small rolling radius compatible with the proposed styling. A more orthodox front sub-frame assembly replaced the old chassis of the Interceptor, while suspension utilised unequal length wishbones supported by low rate dampers and progressive bump stops.

Towns was also involved with styling the F Type's interior which, like the rest of the car, was to incorporate the most modern trim and fittings. In fact, William Towns now says that when he later became involved with the design of Aston Martin's latest Lagonda, some of this ideas for the F Type were used again. At the time, Jensen were testing out a particular type of Lucas 'touch' switch for the dashboard, and Towns says that it would have shared the same 'solid state' feel as that of the Lagonda.

In 1974 Jensen launched the Interceptor Convertible. Many of the company's pre-war models were tourers and this car contained the best of Jensen's craftsmanship in open air motoring.

As the F programme moved ahead, one bodyshell was used for roof crush, barrier and side intrusion tests while another was made into the one and only fully running prototype. At MIRA it showed its capabilities and was timed at over 140 mph, the car's maximum speed being tempered only by its axle ratio, the rev. counter showing 5,500 rpm. But the F Type, or Esperado as it was to be called, never moved beyond the prototype stage simply because, in the early 1970s, Interceptor sales were still buoyant at around 30 to 35 per week and the company were also heavily engrossed in the productionising of the Jensen Healey Sports. In the event, time ran out for the F Type and today only two bodyshells remain of this exciting car.

Contrary to many beliefs that the American regulations had rendered the age of the soft top car dead, Jensen's Convertible answered a demand for a convertible car in the executive market.

Two Jensen models of this late period in Jensen's history which did reach production were the Convertible and the Coupé. Much to some people's surprise – for it was popularly thought that the American safety regulations prohibited convertibles – Jensen launched their soft top version of the Interceptor in 1974. Some in-house restyling had changed the rear end of the basic Interceptor shape to accommodate the canvas hood and produce a conventional boot area behind. It immediately became a popular car, despite its £9,863 price tag.

Meanwhile, there had been some changes in personalities on the Jensen Board. Alf Vickers, who had joined the company in 1970, had left in July 1973 and had been replaced as Managing Director by Kevin Beattie. But Beattie, whose health had been weakened some years earlier and who had withstood the tremendous strain of getting the Interceptor and FF into production, as well as maintaining production through the bleak periods of 1968/69, became ill again the following year. Then, in October 1974, he temporarily relinquished his post as MD to Kjell Qvale. Sadly, Kevin Beattie never wholly regained his health and he died in September 1975.

The same year, and while in the hands of the Receiver, Jensen announced on Review Day of the London Motor Show, their latest and last model: the Coupé. With a Panther-designed hard top, which was not detachable, it was a striking car incorporating the notch back of the Convertible with the fixed roof of the basic Interceptor, the roof having tinted glass panels to the top and sides. Some people say it was the best looking Interceptor of all.

The dashboard of an Interceptor Convertible for the American market. The steering wheel has been changed and a veneer panel added to the centre console. (courtesy of J.O.C.)

The rear seats of the Convertible. Only a minimum amount of bracing had to be added to the body to retain its rigidity in convertible form. The hood is power-operated. (courtesy of J.O.C.)

A snowy scene with the Convertible's hood erected against the cold. Rear three quarter vision is obscured by the lack of side windows in the hood.

The Jensen Coupe was the last of the Interceptor range. It was launched at the 1975 Motor Show and featured a fixed hard top with a Convertible-like boot design. Note the modified front grille and the double bumpers. This one is for the States.

Two more views showing the quality and craftsmanship which went into building the Jensen Convertible. Today, they are rare and cherished vehicles which is reflected in their second hand value.

Three views of the Jensen Coupe which belonged to Jensen's PR executive, Tony Good. This particular car was finished by Jensen Parts and Service after Jensen's crash. It features the latest modifications which were made to the Interceptor range including a full walnut dashboard.

Chapter Four

PRAISE IN PRINT

Predictably, the Interceptor generated an enormous amount of interest among automotive journalists, and the motoring press for the period contains a mine of information for those absorbed with the progress of this marque.

'Very satisfying high-performance touring car with practical seating for four plus luggage,' was how *Autocar* described the Interceptor in the introduction to their full road test in January 1967; while *Motor* summed up the car in their road test report with phrases of glowing praise: '...superb engine and transmission...tremendous performance...well balanced handling...comfortable armchair seats...'

The dashboard layout of the Mk 1 Interceptor showing the many different switches and knobs on the centre console. Magazines found the layout confusing. (courtesy of Autocar)

The interior of the Interceptor Mk 11. Its saloon-like capability of taking four people in extreme comfort was highly praised.

As a publicity exercise, Jensen built the Interceptor 'Topic' in conjunction with the Topic Magazine Group. Road tested by John Ball, he said of the car. 'Its acceleration is really something to be experienced.'

The interior of an early Interceptor Mk 11 showing the re-designed dashboard with its extra ventilation sockets. (courtesy of Ian Orford)

With the increasingly stringent safety regulations coming from America, Jensen introduced this dashboard on all their models from 1971. Note the crash padding on the steering wheel and the four ventilation sockets.
(courtesy of Ian Orford)

Motor went on to say that, 'Even on part throttle, the Interceptor can normally out-accelerate anything in sight with that silken surge so typical of a big V-8.' Not that the Mk I Interceptor was designed as a sports saloon, but with 325 bhp at 4,600 rpm (gross) under the bonnet it did accelerate very quickly and *Motor* took the trouble to make acceleration runs using both automatic changes and holding D1 and D2, the magic 60 mph coming up in 8.3 seconds using the first technique and a second less with the latter. 'For more urgent spurts of acceleration,' they explained, 'you flick the lever back to 1 or 2, depressing a button in the top of the lever to do so, and then divert attention to the rev. counter needle which swings round to 5,100 rpm – 53 mph in first, 90 mph in second – with astonishing rapidity.'

However, an area which did come in for some criticism was the heating and ventilation system for, as *Motor* pointed out, there were no fewer than twenty-four different operations the driver could make to regulate it. Clearly, it was a system which was both too complex and confusing. 'Although versatile with separate hot and cold supplies at the front and two blowers to demist the huge back window, it did not function efficiently and we found temperature control insensitive,' said *Autocar*.

As for the Jensen FF, which was awarded 'Car of the Year' by *Car* magazine, L.J.K. Setright got to grips with the four-wheel-drive monster in *Car*, December 1966. 'You can't really tell what the FF is all about just by jumping in and driving it,' he said. 'The thing has to be worked up to gradually and in a scientific manner, getting first this variable and then that evaluated so to acquire some sort of 'control' or norm by which to evaluate the ultimate.'

It was the sheer size (15' 11" long and 5' 10" wide) of the FF with its performance, road holding and Maxaret anti-lock braking which gave the car its reputation. 'Performance with safety' was how *Motor* described the Jensen FF and hailed it as the 'best handling car of its size and power we have tested'. Some fifteen years on it is still difficult not to be

The Autocar team admire the under bonnet arrangement of the FF. To test the car's ability to climb slippery surfaces, they put it on a 1-in-4 ski slope, which it managed to climb! (courtesy of Autocar)

impressed by the words written about the FF. 'At 100 mph the engine is humming unobtrusively at less than 4,000 rpm making the Jensen one of the most restful cars we have ever tested.' But with a retail price of £5,788, or approximately £1,500 more than that of the normal Interceptor, the FF owner should have reasonably expected something special. And that is just what he got. In an attempt to give some measure of the FF's sure footedness, even when the car was driven very hard *Motor* commented, 'Lifting off when cornering hard creates a mild degree of tuck-in which the hardest likely combination of simultaneous braking and cornering does little to aggravate into anything worse than an easily controllable change of line.' As for *Car* magazine, they put it this way, 'What we implied but did not say was that there are *no* cars of equal size and weight and versatility which will hold the road as well, let alone better (than the FF),' and went on to say, 'Usually it is your nerve which fails before the car's cornering power.'

In contrast, the Maxaret anti-skid braking system met with less than enthusiastic response from the motoring journalists. The system's concept was new on a production motor car and, judging from the reports, the equipment fitted to the FF may well have benefitted from more development. *Motor* decided to try the system out with the following results: 'On smooth roads we gained enough confidence in the system to attempt in the dry a brutal panic stop from 120 mph – which in any normal car would have ended in a hospital ward if not the mortuary – to find that the car was brought to a controlled if rather bouncy stop without any skidding or loss of directional control.' On the Maxaret braking equipment the sensing devices detected when the wheels were about to lock and then caused a reverse action of the servo unit which resulted in the brake pedal kicking back against the driver's foot. This 'kick-back' action was found to be un-nerving to the testers and particularly the rate at which movement took place. 'While we are fully converted to the advantages of four-wheel-drive,' said *Autocar*, 'we must retain our reservations about the Maxaret anti-lock braking system.'

The Jensen FF being put through its paces. The press were unanimous about the car's outstanding handling and tractability.

Car magazine's Leonard Setright, puts the Jensen FF through its paces. So impressed was he of the car's technicalities that he said, one tended to take the shape for granted.

L.J.K. Setright and Jensen's Chief Engineer, Kevin Beattie in deep discussion about the Jensen and the merits of the FF. It won the 'Car of the Year' award for 1967.

Testing a Chrysler V8 engine to destruction.
The unit was run at 5000 rpm for 30 hours before a big end bearing collapsed. Such testing is done for the
benefit of the customer and the press. (courtesy of Ian Orford)

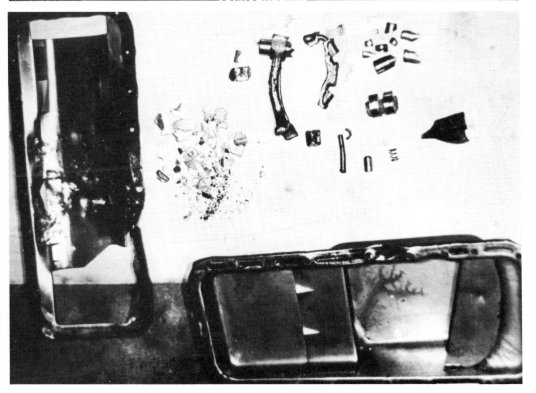

Jensen models always seem to win good praise from American magazines and the Convertible proved particularly popular with its quality and craftsmanship singled out for comment.

Although the Interceptor Mk I was an impressive car which attracted favourable comments from the motoring press, there were some areas for improvement. With the introduction of the Mk II, some minor changes were made to the suspension and the tyres were changed to radial ply. But the main area of improvement was to the interior. 'The seats are new and entirely improved,' said *Autocar*. As for the dashboard, the important news here was that it had been completely re-designed with better instrumentation, and rocker switches replaced the previous toggle type. The ventilation system, too, was improved with more outlets on the facia. 'Clearly, though, the Jensen's main point is that even without its options it is still a very completely equipped vehicle,' commented *Autocar*.

In January 1971 *Sports Car Graphic* tried a Jensen Interceptor Mk II and said, 'For any price this Jensen just doesn't hardly do anything wrong under *any* conditions,' (sic.) and carried on to say, 'Perhaps it is happenstance (sic.) and possibly it comes from years of hard work, but the Jensen comes across with finely tuned and well developed suspension/tyre/chassis that gives a superb combination of a just-right ride and secure handling.' *Sports Car Graphic* completed their Interceptor test by saying. 'Yes, reader, take heed. Considering all the five-figure luxury performance cars we have tested, the Jensen is the first one to seem functionally and esthetically (sic.) worth its tag. Still, at a formidably grandiose $13,500... "To dream the impossible dream..."

With Jensen's limited production quanitites, costly development could not be considered and it was not until the introduction of the MK 111 cars that the majority of the criticisms had been eliminated. (courtesy of J.O.C.)

For many Jensen enthusiasts the most dramatic of all Interceptor models was the SP version. Standing for Six Pack, the SP (Jensen's flagship to replace the technically brilliant FF) was not only a very fast motor car, it also featured many of the Interceptor's 'optional extra' features (such as air conditioning) as standard equipment. In fact, while the Interceptor still came fitted with the 6.3 litre Chrysler engine, the SP sported the larger 7.2 litre unit. However, as *Motor* pointed out in their road test in March 1972, 'In terms of specific output it isn't a particularly efficient unit with only 330 bhp from over 7 litres, but it develops this at only 4,800 rpm and its maximum torque of 410 lb. ft. at 3,600 rpm.' On the road the SP produced a 0 to 60 mph time of 7.6 seconds in either automatic or manual select form, while maximum speed was just over 140 mph. In fact, it wasn't until later that *Motor* realised that 'their' car had a faulty engine which obviously had an adverse effect on its performance figures. As for handling, however, *Motor* declared, 'In comparative terms the roadholding is good and you find that your favourite corners taken fast in a Lotus Elan can be taken nearly as fast in the Jensen.' Praise indeed.

When *Sports Car World* tested an SP in September 1972 they said, 'If the Jensen SP can be summed up in one word, then that word unquestionably is "relentless". This big, beautiful car seems to flatten hills, ignore bends, smooth out bumps and just keeps pounding on and on.'

Compare this shot with the previous view of a convertible. This car features the latest dashboard layout with walnut veneer. (courtesy of Ian Orford)

In April 1973 John Bolster of *Autosport* road tested a Mk III Interceptor. By now the standard car had inherited the 7.2 litre J Series engine but, with emission control equipment strangling performance, the rated output was reduced to a mere 284 bhp at 4,800 rpm. Surprisingly, this had little effect on the car's acceleration or top speed, with Bolster reaching the magic 60 mph in 6.4 seconds and recording a mean maximum of 140 mph. 'If the design is conventional the execution is superb,' wrote Bolster. 'The body is beautifully made and the standard equipment includes all the extras available on other cars, such as refrigerated air-conditioning.' But high speed driving carried a penalty. As Bolster added, 'The robust construction and the simplicity of the design ensure low maintenance costs, but about 15 mpg is the best you can hope for if you drive fairly fast in England. Cruising at over 100 mph on the Continent, 12 or 13 mpg is more usual, and if you have a long burst at 130 to 140 mph, you had better call at the next filling station.'

Clearly, Interceptors had got better over the years. The high standard of Jensen craftsmanship combined with the policy of improving the breed through steady but gradual development had paid dividends and Bolster was impressed enough to say, 'The pleasure of handling such a beautifully made machine cannot easily be put into words.'

But there was some mild criticism, too. *Motor* were forced to comment that, when driven really hard on bumpy surfaces its handling was significantly outclassed by some of its rivals with more advanced suspension systems such as the Aston Martin V8 or the Porche Carrera.

With Carl Duerr and Kjell Qvale's aggressive export drive, by the early 1970s Jensens were being seen across the world, albeit in small numbers. Their popularity was helped considerably by good reports in foreign motoring magazines. (courtesy of J.O.C.)

In October 1974 *Autocar* tested the Jensen Interceptor Mk III Convertible and found that, 'In most respects the Jensen is a comfortable and convenient car to drive.' The acceleration they found, 'pretty vivid for the size of car'. As for the handling, this was, 'all that might be desired'. And of the braking they commented, 'response is excellent for normal use'. However, although the *Autocar* testers were conscious of a pronounced boom from the exhaust at standstill and noted the noisiness of the limited-slip diff., they concluded fairly by saying, 'There are points which we have felt deserve criticism, but it must be stressed that for the man with a comfortable-enough wallet (both to buy it and to pay the fuel bill), it is a highly enjoyable car.'

For some, the prettiest – although not the fastest – Interceptor was the Coupé, launched in 1975. The silhouette of the Convertible had been retained, replacing the canvas top for steel containing a neat smoked-glass panel. Unfortunately, few magazines road tested this vehicle, but one which did – *Road Test* in December 1976 – referred to it as, 'The ultimate automotive Gucci'. Unfortunately, by 1976 the basic Interceptor design was beginning to show its age: '...the theoretical value of the perfect balance is lost by the incredibly vague power steering and strange suspension, which seemed to combine the worst elements of too-stiff springs and too-soft shocks.' Unbelievably, the magazine seemed to be under the misapprehension that the Jensen Interceptor Coupé was made of glass fibre: '...because underneath its fibre glass, the Jensen is an antique among sports cars...'! However, in their final analysis *Road Test* commented, 'Because whatever its shortcomings – and there are a whole slew of them – the car and its company were at least different, and their extinction raises the grim image of a future devoid of differences, run by and for huge corporations cranking out billions of faceless automobiles.'

Carl Duerr in particular was always thinking of ways in which the Interceptor could get more publicity. Here we see an Interceptor being used at the BSM course for high performance driving. (courtesy of J.O.C.)

Chapter Five

CRISIS LOOMS – AND AFTER

Within a month of the Interceptor's launch at the London Motor Show, both Richard and Alan Jensen retired. Ill-health had plagued them both and they felt it was time to give up and left the Board in November 1966. They had set up the business in 1934, had steered it through crises, and even when they handed over the controlling interests to Norcros in 1958, their influence could still be seen on Jensen products. But the failure of the P66 programme must have been particularly bitter for them because they found themselves over-ruled in their own business.

Kevin Beattie was appointed a Director of the Jensen Board in September 1965 and his long-standing friend, Richard Graves, who had joined Jensen to help with the increasingly important aspect of sales, was also made a Director – in December 1966. Then developments occurred which proved crucial to the company's future. The termination in 1967 of the contracts for producing the Austin Healey and the Sunbeam Tiger put Jensen in a financial position from which they never fully recovered. Motoring historians who have studied Jensen's business potential have criticised the company's almost total reliance on these contracts for its stable economic state, because it is said that the net revenue realised from the sales of C-V8s amounted to only £800 per car. And at a time when only some three cars were sold per week, this was obviously a minor contribution to the company's income.

The interior of the West Bromwich factory of Jensen Motors Ltd. showing C-V8 Mk 111s and Austin Healeys being assembled.

The Sunbeam Tiger was another sub-contract job handled by Jensen. In comparison to approximately 74,000 Healeys, only a little over 7,000 Tigers were made but, both contributed enormously to Jensen's finances.

The engine bay of the Tiger showing the Ford V8 engine. Fitting the Ford power unit into the Alpine's engine bay was a work of art and Jensen spent much time on the Tiger's development.

The car which replaced the Austin Healey. This is the pre-production Jensen-Healey seen at Jensen's factory gates.

The Jensen-Healey on display at Jensen's factory. The original styling had been done by Hugo Poole but, before the car reached production, much of it was re-designed by Jensen's styling studios.

In the early days, the Jensen-Healey got a bad reputation as a result of troubles with its Lotus power unit. These were soon solved and in all over 10,000 Healeys were built in 4 years of manufacture.

A typical advertisement used to promote the Jensen-Healey.

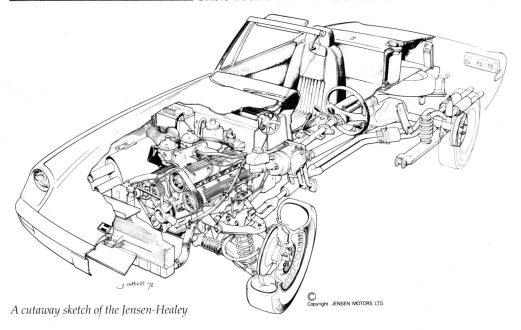

A cutaway sketch of the Jensen-Healey

The 2.0 litre engine made by Lotus for the Jensen-Healey

Tony Good who for many years acted as Jensen's PR executive. He was instrumental in releasing Jensen from Norcros into the hands of Wm. Brandt in 1968.

From L to R: Alf Vickers, Kjell Qvale and Donald Healey at a Press Conference in May 1970. Qvale had just taken over control of the company with Healey as his Chairman and Vickers his Managing Director.

One way in which 'Turnaround Man' Carl Duerr used to bring Jensen to the attention of wealthy clients was to use a team of lady demonstrators. He also gave endless interviews and was always on hand to show clients round the factory.

Some views of the Jensen factory and the cars which Qvale bought. (courtesy of Ian Orford)

Complete body/chassis units on their trolleys waiting to be fitted with their power train and running gear.

Interceptors waiting to be fitted with their power units. The engines can be seen lined up on the left of the picture.

An Interceptor already fitted with its front suspension.

Cars up on the gantry with their suspension already fitted, together with their road wheels.

A later shot showing Convertibles in their final state of build-up before being taken for their first road test.

The final check and test area where the cars were brought before being dispatched to dealers and waiting customers.

"We,the undersigned,would like to complain about the disgraceful lack of Jensens."

A novel advertisement complaining about the lack of Jensen cars. At its height, Interceptor production never exceeded more than 35 cars per week.

Jensen were quite unprepared for the sudden loss of their sub-contract work and were forced to reduce their staff from around 1400 people to about 400. Their £3m turnover in 1966, which produced a profit of £183,000, was turned into a £52,000 deficit in 1967. Understandably, Norcros became somewhat concerned about Jensen's future. So much so, that one Board member was forced to ask Managing Director John Sheffield if he felt that it was in the best interests of Norcross to retain their links with Jensen.

Norcros' answer was to release Managing Director Brian Owen from the Jensen Board and replace him with a consulting Managing Director, Carl Duerr. 'The late 1950s and early 1960s saw the emergence of an industrial conglomerate called the holding company,' said Tony Good, Jensen's public relations expert. 'The criticism of this sort of set-up was that it was just a way of buying up totally unrelated companies and putting them together. All the time they were working well and making a profit, all was well. But what happened when they went wrong? There was never any expert at Board level to help out the particular company in trouble. So rather than get labelled with this sort of criticism, Norcros brought in Carl Duerr.'

Norcros approached Booz, Allen & Hamilton, a firm of management consultants, to advise on Jensen's situation and they in turn got in touch with Intercounsel Establishment of Liechtenstein of which Carl Duerr was a partner. Duerr had been Allied Chief of Industry in Austria at the end of WWII and had remained in Europe developing his own inventions and helping companies just like Jensen to get back on the road to recovery. When he first looked at Jensen's problems he had never heard of the company but felt that there was an opportunity to put his theories into practice.

When Duerr arrived at Jensen in January 1968 he found there were several major problems which needed immediate attention. In broad terms, problem number one was to further reduce the workforce while at the same time increasing productivity. This needed the support of the unions involved, and after Duerr had carefully explained the situation, they agreed to co-operate.

The other major issue confronting Duerr when he took office was that of finance and revenue. Duerr had to prove to the shareholders and the suppliers that Jensen were a viable proposition. The order book and assets at the beginning of 1968 were estimated to be worth £500,000 as a going business, but almost nothing if they crashed. Equally important was the job of improving Jensen's image to the outside world so that

The Mk 11 Jensen-Healey with 5 mph bumpers. They did little to help the car's looks and few people can have been involved in 5 mph accidents driving Jensen-Healeys. (courtesy of J.O.C.)

prospective customers did not feel that they were buying a car from an unstable company. That Duerr's hard work and radical approach was successful can be gauged from the fact that by 1969 Interceptor production had increased to between 14-15 units per week, and almost all of these were for the home market. But Duerr was convinced that both the home and European markets could absorb about twenty cars per week and the American market as many again.

But Duerr's job was not just about getting production back on a profitable footing. His other task was to begin looking for a company which would be prepared to take over Jensen from Norcros. As it turned out, the solution came from Tony Good of the company's public relations consultants, Good Relations. One of Tony Good's other interest was in an investment company called Assets in Action and together they devised a scheme: the Merchant Bankers, Wm. Brandts, were to buy the entire Jensen equity and then pass over forty per cent of this to Duerr and some other Jensen Directors. In June 1968 this plan was put into operation and at the time the Jensen Board comprised Duerr, Tony Good, Kevin Beattie and Richard Graves, with a nomine Chairman, Frank Welsh, who was put in by Brandts.

Just over eighteen months after Duerr arrived at West Bromwich, Jensen produced their 1,000th Interceptor and total sales for that year amounted to 500 units. The significance of the 1,000 cars was that they had been built in less than three years and represented more than the total of all other Jensens built since the company had been established. Yet, despite these encouraging signs, the situation at Jensen was still far from good. To begin with, Duerr's unconventional approach to projecting Jensen's image – which was done largely on a personal level – had tended to antagonise certain people within the company.

The Jensen GT, built largely to satisfy a market in America which was demanding a four seater tourer with the same quality as the Interceptor, but cheaper to run.

Two views of the William Towns styled G Type which was to have taken over from the Jensen GT, had it reached production.

By the mid 1970s, the under bonnet view of a Jensen Interceptor looked like this. Inevitably, reliability suffered and maintenance became more difficult. (courtesy of Ian Orford)

It seems he was the sort of man about whom everyone had a definite opinion (good or bad), although as Tony Good was to explain later, 'I think Carl Duerr was the right man for the job at the time because the business needed to be turned around and the workforce needed to be motivated. If anything, it was Jensen's Board structure at the time which was weak and this put too much strain on Duerr's shoulders, although there were some people at Jensen who felt that his dynamic approach was unsuitable and were sensitive about the company being seen to be run by one man.'

Behind the scenes, Jensen's financial position was also causing concern, not only among the Board members but also with Wm. Brandts. This was 1969 and a credit squeeze was just about to begin. Bankers had worried looks on their faces and company directors were calling for retrenchment programmes to keep their businesses functioning. Brandts were less than happy about Jensen's financial situation and called in their own company consultant, Alf Vickers, to help sort out the problem.

Vickers was born in 1917 and had spent the early part of his life around the Yorkshire collieries and iron foundaries in the North of England. He then went to Manchester University before joining Rolls-Royce, where he became Deputy Technical Production Manager at the early age of 23. Later, he moved to Trafford Park, Manchester to become Technical Production Manager of Ford's Merlin engine factory. He was 25 years old. With the war over he started his own business making metal window frames and in four years it became one of the biggest firms of its kind in the country. In 1951, he returned to Rolls-Royce at their East Kilbridge site before moving into the world of crane construction. It was after leaving this work and going into freelance consultancy that he met up with William Brandts.

The P66 (in hard top form), and a Mk 1 Interceptor about to leave the factory for delivery to a dealer. Compare the styling of the two cars. Had the P66 gone into production, it would have only delayed the launch of a C-V8 replacement still further.

The last car to leave Jensen Motors Limited. Above it is a heartfelt message from those who built it. (courtesy of Ian Orford)

But, Jensen the name and model live on in the form of Jensen Parts and Service. The compay has been set up in the old servicing section of Jenson Motors Ltd. and these photographs show the servicing and restoration work which goes on to keep Jensen cars on the road.

'My consultancy work,' said Vickers, 'was done in conjunction with merchant bankers such as Hambro's who had invested in companies which subsequently lost money. I would then be put in as a nominee director to study the problems and put right whatever was wrong, whether it be marketing, sales or the product. It was 1969 and I had been introduced to William Brandts who had owned Jensen Motors for about eighteen months and had just received the first set of figures. These showed a deficit of £360,000 and a stock deficit of £80,000 which put the company in a very serious position. In fact, it was almost insolvent. Jensen were losing about £40,000 per month.'

Like Duerr, Vickers felt that the image projected by Jensen to the outside world was good. The product was right and the company still maintained a very high reputation. The key factor to the company's weakness was its internal organization. 'There were two main reasons why Jensen were in this state,' continued Vickers. 'To begin with, their overheads were too high. Then there was the organization of the labour force. This was geared to building fifteen cars per week, but in fact they were only building about eleven, and of these only about eight were actually being sold. In addition, there was a wasteful deployment of staff: highly skilled men were being used to produce parts which required only average ability. The equipment was old and the time taken to produce each part was too long.'

With a less than enthusiastic report Vickers went back to Brandts. As he now recalls, 'It was difficult that Duerr was still there, but he accepted the situation. The week after I completed my report and returned to the company as General Manager, Duerr left for Germany.'

'The first think I had to do,' continued Vickers, 'was to arrange for a thirty-three per cent redundancy, as well as renegotiate the bonus schemes because the old ones were so calculated that, had the company built more than fifteen cars per week, it would have gone broke.

'For the company to function at all I had to guarantee a sale of fifteen Interceptors per week and it was on these figures that I based all my other calculations. I knew that Kjell Qvale was in the process of negotiating with Donald Healey over the production of a replacement sports car for the defunct Austin Healey, and I suddenly realised that Jensen Motors Limited was possibly the only company in the UK with the capability and resources to make the new sports car at the rate Qvale required – which was between 150 to 200 units per week.'

Vickers contacted Qvale in San Francisco to outline his plans, saying he could only guarantee that Jensen would remain in business in they sold fifteen cars per week. And if Qvale, with his American-based showrooms, absorbed around five Interceptors per week, Jensen would not only be able to stay in business, they would also be able to manufacture the new Healey sports car which Qvale so desperately needed for his US market. Qvale agreed.

In April 1970, after a series of meetings, it was finally decided that Kjell Qvale would take over Carl Duerr's shares, plus some of those held by William Brandts, so ending up with eighty-four per cent of Jensen Motors Limited. Qvale's new Jensen Board consisted of himself as President, Donald Healey as Chairman, Alf Vickers as Managing Director, as well as Kevin Beattie, Tony Good, Richard Graves and Geoffrey Healey.

However, an area which was still causing Vickers some concern was that of the Interceptor's production quality. But, with his reduced labour force, he introduced strict quality control and a programme to uprate the areas where craftsmanship was lacking. Very soon, production was up to around eighteen cars per week with a smaller labour force that that which had hitherto made only eleven.

This improvement in output and quality encouraged Qvale to buy the balance of Brandt's equity in Jensen, which meant that the merchant bankers had got back every penny they had put in. During the financial year 1970/71 Alf Vickers announced that Jensen had made a profit of £100,000, but this upturn in the company's fortunes was to be short lived for by 1971/72 Jensen began to run into difficulties with productionising the Jensen-Healey sports car.

Alf Vickers left Jensen Motors Limited in 1973. 'The reason I left was that I never intended to stay a managing director of any company for a long period of time,' he said. 'I had achieved what I set out to do and that was that, in the first year of my management, the company should go from deficit to profit.' Alf Vickers' departure was a sad day for Jensen because his considerable expertise in both man management and business operation had been a steadying influence.

To some people it now seemed that Jensen Motors Limited were becoming new model mad. Foremost in this new model programme was the development of a wedge-shaped replacement for the Interceptor, code named the F Type. But, as Vickers remembers, the panel tooling alone would have cost between £1½m and £2m. 'And then we had a drophead version of the Interceptor and a GT version of the Healey on the stocks, all being designed by a team of between four and six people, as well as a production engineering department. They just did not seem to appreciate the tremendous costs of productionising any new car. The Interceptor was only as good as it was because of the considerable amount of development spread over a number of years.'

It seem there two schools of thought at Jensen Motors during this period: those who felt that Interceptor production should be maintained while developing the Jensen-Healey, and those who wanted to increase the Jensen range. In addition to the Interceptor Convertible there were plans for a Coupé version of the Interceptor *and* a mid-range gull-wing car (code named the G Type) to slot between the Jensen-Healey and the F Type. As Alf Vickers was to say later, 'Towards the end of my time there, the company had more new projects in the pipeline than even BL had at the time!'

The world recession occasioned by the oil crisis of 1973/74 was a shock to the British economy but a disaster for firms like Jensen. Added to the slump in demand for Jensen cars was the unprecedented experience of industrial unrest in the company. Moreover, Jensen was in a highly vulnerable position anyway due to its substantial development programme which had been financially underpinned by Kjell Qvale's personal guaranteed loans.

Drastic cuts in staffing followed. Towards the end of 1974 the *Daily Mail* declared, '400 Workers are to be sacked at Jensen Cars', and of the 1,260 workforce the remaining 800 or so were put on short time. The situation deteriorated rapidly and in 1975 a Receiver was called in. This was sad news for all Jensen employees, but saddest of all for Kjell Qvale whose personal dream had been shattered and whose personal loss was estimated at between £2m-£3m.

Although few observers were optimistic, various efforts were made to rescue the firm until May 1976, when Jensen Motors Limited finally closed.

'There may have been ways in which Jensen could have been saved,' said Tony Good recently. 'I think that, had we talked to different people at the time, the outcome may have been different. But then, the motor industry was going through a particularly tough period which was even affecting Chrysler, General Motors and Ford. But I think that Jensen deserved to survive more than some who did, although I accept that this is a view based on twelve years' close involvement with company.'

According to the Receiver, John Griffiths, Jensen Motors failed for three reasons: expensive engineering required bysafety and emission laws, disappointing sales in the United States, and the high rate of inflation at home. But, perhaps, the final words should come from Ian Orford, whose company, Jensen Parts and Service was created from the ruins of Jensen Motors Limited, and whose workforce have just finished the first all-new 1983 Interceptor: 'If it hadn't been for the Interceptor going into production, we wouldn't be here today.'

Interceptor 83. This car has been built by JP & S for launch at Motorfair 83. Everyone hopes it will be the start of Jensen cars back in production. Let's hope so.

Chapter Six

COMPETITIVE SPIRIT

Despite its performance, the Interceptor was never seen in competitive motor sport in this country during its production life. This lack of sporting background has led the Jensen Owners' Club to concentrate much of its activities on concours events which are held with aggressive enthusiasm at their annual International Weekends. Over a number of years, a handful of Interceptors have emerged as outstanding vehicles of their class and type.

Jensen Interceptor Mk III (J Series) Owned by Peter Adams.

In Peter Adams' own words, his Interceptor is probably the most well known of all because of its number of appearances at shows and events up and down the country. The car, a 1972 model, was in fact used by Jensen's President, Kjell Qvale and, when Jensen Motors Limited crashed in May 1976, was the only car to be transferred to Jensen Parts and Service. Peter had always wanted to buy a new Interceptor but, by the time he was in a position to do so, Jensen had gone into liquidation. However, well-known Jensen man, Dave Horton, told him about Jensen Parts and Service and Peter travelled up to West Bromwich to meet the Sales Director, who gave him a memorable ride in the car he now owns.

The award winning Interceptor 'J' Series of Peter Adams. The car was used by Jensen's boss, Kjell Qvale and was the only complete car to be transferred from Jensen Motors Ltd. to Jensen Parts and Service Ltd. in 1976.

Within a year of buying his Interceptor, Peter had decided to keep the car specifically for entering in shows and concours events, and a list of the car's successes follows:

JENSEN INTERCEPTOR III (J. SERIES)

1977   Awarded 'Best Hard Topped Interceptor' by Jensen Owners Club.

1978   Awarded 'Best Interceptor' by the Jensen Owners Club.
Awarded Best Overall Jensen' (Presidents Cup), by Jensen Owners Club.
Awarded 'Best Jensen Interceptor' by the Jensen Factory.
Member of the winning team Alexandra Palace.
1st in Class – Air Touring Class Car & Historic Aircraft Show, Biggin Hill August.

1979   Gained 1st place in Class at Biggin Hill International Air Fair May.
Received Sir Douglas Bader Trophy.
Presented by Raymond Baxter of B.B.C. Television.
Featured in Auto Car Magazine May.
Gained 2nd place (joint) visitors choice Jensen Owners Club National Weekend 15th-17th June.
Received Special Concours Award as a Masters Class Car Jensen National Weekend.
Gained 2nd Class Airtouring Rally of Classic Cars & Historic Aircraft 28/29th July.
Gained 1st Class, Battle of Britain Day, Biggin Hill, September. This award was presented by His Royal Highness King Hussein of Jordan.

1980   Featured in a national advertising campaign by Messrs. P.J. Langford March.
Awarded 3rd place at Jensen International Weekend with same marks as 1st & 2nd place cars.
Received Special Masters Class Award from Club. Awarded 'Best Interceptor'.
Represented Jensen Owners' Club in Team section of Bromley Pageant of Motoring – Received 1st in Class.
Featured in special edition of Brooklands Books.

1981   Represented Jensen Onwers' Club at Bromley Pageant of Motoring – 3rd in Team Award Class
Received Special Masters Class Award from Jensen Owners' Club at International Weekend – Awarded 'Best Interceptor'.

1982   Represented Jensen Owners' Club at Farnborough Fair International Lions May 9th. Received award from Mayor of Bromley. (Round Table Charity)
Represented Jensen Owners' Club in the Promley Pageant of Motoring – 1st in Class. Team entry concours.
Featured in 50th Commemorative edition of Jensen Owners' Club National Magazine with colour feature.
Represented Jensen Owners' Cub at Goodwood Race Track – September 22nd. Thoroughbred & Classic Car Press Day.
Represented Jensen Owners' Club at Thoroughbred & Classic Car Show 3-day Indoor Event – Brighton Metropole.

1983   Featured in Jensen Owners' Club National calendar November/December
Represented Jensen Owners' Club at Press & Test Day Brands Hatch Race Track.
Awarded 1st in Masters Class Jensen Owners' Club at International Weekend Golden Valley Cheltenham.
Awarded Presidents Cup for 'Best Over All Jensen' – Presented by Lord Strathcarron.
Note – No other Jensen in the history of the Club has won the Presidents Cup on more occasions than this car.
Represented the Jensen Owners' Club at Southern Jaguar Day Leeds Castle 24th July.

Norman Long's well known FF Mk 11 on display at Biggin Hill, Kent. In all, only 316 FFs were made making them rare cars among the Jensen range. Norman says he bought this car because it was an FF and because it was white. (courtesy of N. Long)

Jensen FF owned by Norman Long.

Norman 'FF' Long, as he is affectionately known among JOC members, bought his car in March 1975. Such is its rarity, the car is the sixth of only one hundred and ten made. At the time of purchase, though, he paid only £1,600 for it, which gives some idea of how the market value had dropped at that time.

Norman says that his primary interest is the car's four-wheel-drive layout and anti-skid braking, although he does concede that the car's colour – which is white – was a factor in his buying this particular one because he feels the colour suits the shape.

Norman has always tried to keep his FF as original as possible and says he thinks it is possibly the best FF in the country. A shortened list of the car's awards is as follows:

Since joining the JOC in 1976, the car has won the Best FF Award every year.

Overall winner	J.P. & Service Concours 1978
Best FF	J.P. & Service Concours 1979
2nd in class	Brighton & Hove Concours D'Elegance 1978
2nd in class	Brighton & Hove Concours D'Elegance 1979
	Has represented the JOC at all the Alexandra Palace and
	Thoroughbred & Classic Car Shows, always in the winning teams.

This is the Jensen SP of Peter Sbardella, which has been seen at a great many club events and national shows. Peter bought the car in 1976 – the fulfilment of a dream – and since then its preparation for Concour events has been taken care of by his daughter, Lisa. (courtesy of P Sbardella)

Jensen SP owned by Peter Sbardella.

As a young man, Peter always dreamed of owning a Jensen and, when the opportunity came in 1976, he was not disappointed. The car's sleek, graceful lines combined with the brutal performance from its 'Six Pack' engine more than fulfil that dream. He loves driving the car.

From the beginning, the car has been prepared for events by his daughter, Lisa, and was entered in its first concours by mistake at the Jensen National Day at Woburn Abbey in 1977. Below are listed some of the awards and appearances Peter's SP has made over the years:

1st	Sandwell Historic Vehicle Parade 1980 J.P. & Service Trophy
1st in class	Brighton & Hove Concourse D'Elegance 1980
1st in class	Bromley Pageant of Motoring 1980 Jensen Owners' Club 1980 Masters Class Award
1st	Sandwell Historic Vehicle Parade 1981 J.P. & Service Trophy

1st	International Air Fair 1981 Team Event
2nd	Masters Class, Jensen Owners' Club International Weekend 1981
1st	Members Choice, Jensen Owners' Club Concours 1981
1st	Sandwell Historic Vehicle Parade 1982 J.P. & Service Trophy
2nd in class	Brighton & Hove Concours D'Elegance 1982
1st in class	Jensen Owner's Club International Concours 1982
1st	Members Choice, Jensen Owners' Club International Concours 1982
3rd in class	The National Classic Car Concours Knebworth 1982
1st	Sandwell Historic Vehicle Parade 1983 J.P. & Service Trophy
2nd in class	Brighton & Hove Concours D'Elegance 1983
1st	Members Choice, Jensen Owners' Club Internation Concours 1983
2nd in class	The National Classic Car Concours Knebworth 1983

This is Mike Lotwis, who must surely be one of the most well known Jensen enthusiasts in America, seen here with his Mk 111 Interceptor.

And, just to prove that Jensens do compete in competitive motorsport, here is Mike thrashing his Interceptor round the course of an American rally.

SPECIFICATIONS

	UK list price	Average fuel consumption (mpg)	Speed in the gears			Acceleration (secs)			
			3	2	1	0-30	40	50	60
Interceptor Mk 1	£3743	13.6	133	92	54	3.3	4.3	5.9	7.3
Interceptor Mk 11	£5198	12.9	137	95	55	2.5	3.7	5.0	6.4
Jensen SP	£6977	14.0	143	99	59	2.9	4.1	5.4	6.9
C-V8 Mk 111	£3491	13.2	130	88	52	2.8	4.0	5.0	6.7
FF	£6017	14.0	130	88	52	3.1	4.4	6.2	8.4
FF Mk 11	£7705	14.0	141	93	55	3.5	4.8	6.2	8.1
Convertible	£9683	12.0	126	87	52	2.7	4.0	5.5	7.6
Coupé	£11758	11.0	130	73	38	3.6	4.9	7.0	9.6
Aston Martin V8 (automatic)	£9592	12.4	147	108	64	2.6	3.7	4.8	6.2

70	80	90	100	bhp	torque	cc	road test
.5	12.1	15.4	19.0	325 @ 4,600 (gross)	425 @ 2,800 (gross)	6,276	Autocar 5.1.67
.7	11.2	14.3	18.2	330 @ 4,600 (SAE)	425 @ 2,800 (gross)	6,276	Autocar 4.9.69
.9	11.1	13.5	16.8	330 @ 4,700 (net)	490 @ 3,200 (gross)	7,212	Autocar 7.10.71
.5	10.9	13.9	17.6	330 @ 4,600 (gross)	425 @ 2,800 (gross)	6,276	Autocar 16.4.65
.8	13.8	17.5	22.5	325 @ 4,600 (gross)	425 @ 2,800 (gross	6,276	Autocar 28.3.68
.6	13.4	16.7	21.5	330 @ 5,000 (SAE)	425 @ 2,800 (SAE)	6,276	Autocar 22.10.70
.8	12.5	15.8	20.2	280 @ 4,800 (net)	380 @ 3,200 (net)	7,212	Autocar 26.10.74
.2	16.2			215 @ 5,200	330 @ 3,200	7,212	Road Test Dec. 76
.2	10.2	12.7	15.7	Not quoted	Not quoted	5,340	Autocar 6.9.73

SPECIFICATION

1/27

A 23½″
B 2″
C 37—42″
D 36″
E 17—22″
F 16″
G 30″
H 38″

ENGINE. Chrysler 90° Vee 8, O.H.V. with hydraulic tappets.

Standard engine
Bore 3.63 in. (92.5 mm)
Stroke 3.31 in. (84.1 mm)
Cubic capacity 273 cu. in. (4475 cc)
Compression Ratio 10.5 : 1

Alternative engine (available at extra cost)
Bore 4.25 in. (108 mm)
Stroke 3.38 in. (86 mm)
Cubic capacity 383 cu. in. (6276 cc)
Compression Ratio 10 : 1

Crankshaft. Fully balanced. 5 main bearings. Fitted with torsional vibration damper. Lubrication System. Externally mounted rotor type pump with combined full flow filter. Paper element.
Fuel System. Mechanical pump. In line 'throw away' filter. Carter 4 barrel carburetter with automatic thermostatically controlled choke. Paper element carburetter air cleaner. Twin fuel tanks total capacity 20 Imp. galls. (91 litres). Lockable quick release fuel filler cap.
Ignition. Dual phased contact breaker points. Automatic and vacuum advance. Ballast resistor for initial spark boost.

SUSPENSION.
Front. Independent coil and wishbone with lever type shock absorbers.
Rear. De Dion tube; semi-elliptic springs with telescopic shock absorbers.

COOLING. High pressure (14 lb. sq. in. .948 Kg/cm²) system with pellet type thermostat. Twin thermostatically controlled electric cooling fans.

TRANSMISSION.
Automatic. Torquefire (Hi performance) 3 speed automatic transmission with torque converter. Overriding hold controls and kickdown on 1st and 2nd gears. Central control with illumirated indicator. Parking lock.

Overall ratios:
1st 8.10 : 1   3rd 3.31 : 1
2nd 4.80 : 1   Reverse 7.28 : 1
Transmission oil cooler incorporated in radiator bottom tank.

Manual.
Overall ratios:
1st 8.80 : 1   Top 3.31 : 1
2nd 6.32 : 1   Reverse 8.54 : 1
3rd 4.60 : 1
Hydraulically operated S.D.P. clutch. Open propeller shaft.
Hypoid final drive. Ratio 3.31 : 1.

STEERING.
Forward mounted high efficiency rack and pinion incorporating dash pot dampers. Greaseless steering joints. Ball type swivel bearings. 17″ wood rimmed wheel on adjustable column. 3.3 turns lock to lock.

BRAKES. Hydraulically operated self adjusting Dunlop disc brakes on all 4 wheels. Separate systems for front and rear brakes with tandem master cylinder and servo assistance. Swept area 498 sq. in. (3213 cm²). Floor mounted lever to the right of drivers seat operates separate self adjusting parking brakes on rear wheel.

SAFETY BELTS. Diagonal belts to both front seats.

ELECTRICAL EQUIPMENT.
12 volt alternator with 6 silicon rectifiers. Voltage regulator. Battery 74 a/h. 7″ sealed beam headlights with flasher switch incorporated in turn indicator control. Side, rear and number plate lights. Dual intensity instrument lighting. Two speed electric windscreen wipers with anti-lifting blades. Electric screenwashers. Reversing light operated by switch incorporated in gear selector mechanism. Self cancelling turn indicators with warning light.

INSTRUMENTS.
Speedometer. Impulse type tachometer. Ammeter, oil pressure gauge. Fuel gauge. Coolant temperature gauge. Warning lights for high beam and low fuel.

HEATING AND VENTILATION.
Heating. Fresh air 4 Kw heater incorporating windscreen demister/defroster and two speed booster fan. High level air intake. Ventilation. Individually controlled fresh air outlets at face level and into footwells.

WHEELS AND TYRES. Ventilated disc wheels with tubed Dunlop 6.40 x 15 R.S. tyres.

JACKING SYSTEM. Bevelift type system operating with easily accessible lifting points.

SPARE WHEEL. In special easily accessible carrier on boot floor.

LEADING DIMENSIONS.
Overall length 14′8″
Overall width 5′9″
Overall height 4′3″
Wheelbase 102″
Track front 54″
Track rear 54¾″
Ground clearance 6½″
Turning circle 37½′
Weight 25 cwt.

BODY. All aluminium mounted on perimeter type tubular chassis giving 2/4 seater accommodation. P.V.C. upholstery over foam. Front seats adjustable for rake and with quick release for access to rear. One rear seat collapsible for additional space if required. Pockets in both doors and rear quarter panels. Fully convertible with P.V.C. topping on light alloy frame. Hard top available at extra cost.
We reserve the right to alter specification or equipment without notice

JENSEN MOTORS LTD.
West Bromwich, England. Tel: West Bromwich 2041 (10 lines)

NORCROS GROUP

A	25″	E	21″
B	2″	F	20″
C	39″ - 44″	G	36″
D	36″	H	36″

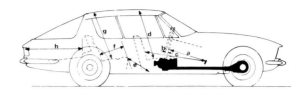

It is not a new car. It is a new kind of car. Under the sleekly power-packed lines of the Jensen FF is the formula for the future.

Once again Jensen Motors are first to lead the way towards finer cars—but this time the innovation is a gigantic step into the future, even by Jensen standards. The Jensen FF with its revolutionary 4-wheel drive and aviation developed anti-skid braking system, blends speed and safety as never before. Here is a car which can be driven as no car has ever been driven.

The Jensen FF opens a new era in motoring—an era of faster, safer driving. Driving the Jensen FF is an electrifying experience. It gives the motorist comfort, relaxation and a new kind of confidence.

SPECIFICATION

ENGINE:

Chrysler 90° Vee 8, O.H.V. with hydraulic tappets.

Bore	4.25 in. (108 mm)
Stroke	3.38 in. (86 mm)
Cubic capacity	383 cu. in. (6276 cc)
Compression ratio	10:1

Crankshaft. Fully balanced, 5 main bearings. Fitted with torsional vibration damper.

Lubrication System: Externally mounted rotor type pump with combined full flow filter. Paper element.

Fuel System: Mechanical Pump. Filter in fuel line. Carter 4 barrel carburettor with automatic thermostatically controlled choke. Flashing low fuel-level warning light operative below 3 gallons (13 litres). Tank capacity 16 Imp. gallons (72 litres). Large capacity paper element air cleaner.

Ignition: Automatic and vacuum advance. Ballast resistor for initial spark boost.

SUSPENSION:

Front. Independent. Wishbones with double combined spring/damper units.

Rear. Semi-elliptic dual rate springs with rubber button inter-leaved separators. Armstrong telescopic driver controlled adjustable dampers. Panhard rod.

COOLING:

High pressure (14 lb. sq. in. .948 Kg/cm²) system with pellet type thermostat. Twin thermostatically controlled electric cooling fans.

TRANSMISSION:

Torqueflite 3 speed automatic transmission with torque converter. Overriding hold controls and kickdown on first and second gears. Floor mounted control with illuminated indicator. Transmission oil cooler incorporated in radiator bottom tank.

Overall ratios.

1st	7.50	Top	3.07
2nd	4.44	Reverse	6.75

Ferguson Formula 4 wd unit. Open propeller shafts. Hypoid final drive units, axle ratio 3.07:1.

STEERING:

Power assisted. Ratio 13.7:1. 2.57 turns lock to lock. Turning circle 39 ft.

BRAKES:

Hydraulically operated self-adjusting disc brakes on all 4 wheels. Separate systems for front and rear brakes with booster assisted tandem master cylinder and incorporating Dunlop Maxaret anti-skid device. Swept area 498.2 sq. ins. (32.4 cm²). Central handlever operates self-adjusting parking brakes on rear wheels.

SAFETY BELTS:

Standard to both front seats.

ELECTRICAL EQUIPMENT

12 volt 40 amp alternator with 6 silicon rectifiers. Voltage regulator. Battery 67 a/h. Twin sealed beam headlights with flasher switch incorporated in turn indicator control. Side and rear lights, number plate, engine compartment and boot illumination lights. Rheostat controlled instrument light. Interior light with courtesy switches on doors. Rear interior lights with combined switches.

Twin bladed two-speed self parking electric windscreen wipers with anti-lifting blades and screen washers. Illuminated cigar lighter. Reversing lights operated by switch incorporated in gear selector mechanism. Illuminated electric clock. Self-cancelling turn indicators with warning lights. Electrically operated windows. Red warning lights in door trailing edges.

INSTRUMENTS:

Speedometer, electric impulse type tachometer, ammeter, oil pressure and coolant temperature gauges and fuel gauge. Warning lights for high beam, low fuel.

RADIO: Fully transistorised, twin speakers.

HEATING AND VENTILATION:

Heating. Fresh air 4½ Kw unit incorporating windscreen demister/defroster and two speed booster fan. High level air intake. Individual outlets to front and rear foot wells.

Ventilation. Individually controlled fresh air outlets at face level and in front foot wells delivering ambient temperature air. Booster fan in face level system. Electrically heated rear window.

WHEELS AND TYRES:

Disc wheels with tubed Dunlop R.S. 6.70 x 15 tyres which are suitable for sustained speeds of up to 110 m.p.h. without increasing pressure.

JACKING SYSTEM:

Bevelift type system operating in conjunction with special lifting points.

SPARE WHEEL:

In special carrier underneath luggage compartment.

LEADING DIMENSIONS:

Overall length	15ft. 11in.
Overall width	5ft. 9in.
Overall height	4ft. 5in.
Wheelbase	9ft. 1in.
Track front	4ft. 8⅛in.
Track rear	4ft. 8⅛in.
Ground clearance	5⅜in.
Turning circle	39 ft.
Weight	34 cwt.

BODY:

Steel body mounted on a tubular chassis giving full four seater accommodation. Safety belts to both seats which are fitted with finely adjustable reclining hinges incorporating quick release for access to rear seats. Map pockets to both doors. Centre mounted lockable compartment. Covered pockets in rear armrests. 16 cu. ft. (·45 m³) luggage compartment with spring loaded self supporting lid.

We reserve the right to alter details of price, specification or equipment without notice.

JENSEN MOTORS LTD. West Bromwich, England.   Tel. West Bromwich 2041 (10 lines)   CGA/LB 967 5M   a member of the NORCROS GROUP

Specification of Jensen FF

Engine

Chrysler 90° Vee 8, O.H.V. with hydraulic tappets. Bore 4.32 in. Stroke 3.75 in. Cubic Capacity 440 cu. in. (7,212 cc) Compression ratio 8.2 : 1. Crankshaft: Fully balanced, 5 main bearings. Fitted with torsional vibration damper. Lubrication system: Externally mounted rotor type pump with separate full flow filter. Fuel system: Mechanical pump. Filter in fuel line. Four-barrel carburettor with automatic thermostatically controlled choke. Flashing low fuel-level warning light operative below 2½ gallons (Imp.) 13 litres. Tank capacity 20 gallons (Imp.) 91 litres. Large capacity paper element air cleaner. Ignition: Electronic automatic centrifugal and vacuum advance. Ballast resistor for initial spark boost. Cooling: High pressure (13 lb. sq. in.) system with pellet type thermostat. Twin thermo- statically controlled electric cooling fans.

Transmission

Torqueflite Hi-Performance 3-speed automatic with torque converter. Over-riding hold controls, kickdown. Centrally mounted quadrant.
Overall ratios:
1st 7.50 : 1
2nd 4.44 : 1
3rd 3.07 : 1
Reverse 6.74
Transmission oil cooler incorporated in radiator side tank. Open propeller shaft. Hypoid rear axle incorporating 'Powr Lok' limited slip differential. Axle ratio 3.07 : 1.

Suspension

Front: Independent coil and wishbone with telescopic type dampers. Stabiliser bar. Rear: Semi-elliptic dual rate springs with rubber button interleaved separators. Armstrong telescopic dampers, Panhard rod.

Steering

Power assisted. 15 in. diameter leather covered steering wheel with 2 in. reach adjustment. 3.4 turns lock to lock: 17.1 : 1 ratio. Turning circle 38 ft. steering column lock.

Wheels and tyres

Aluminium alloy cast wheels with Dunlop ER 70 VR15 tubed tyres suitable for sustained speeds up to 110 mph without increasing pressure. Spare wheel in carrier underneath luggage compartment.

Brakes

Hydraulically operated self-adjusting Girling ventilated disc brakes on all four wheels. Separate systems for front and rear brakes with tandem master cylinder and servo assistance. Load conscious valve in rear system to prevent rear wheel lock-up. Swept area 417 sq. in. Central hand lever operates self-adjusting brakes on rear wheels. Brake pad wear indicator.

Electric equipment

12 volt 65 amp alternator with 6 silicon rectifiers. Transistorised voltage regulator. Battery 66 a/h.

Four 5¾ in. Quartz halogen headlights. Side, and Dual Intensity rear lights. Reversing light operated by switch incorporated in gear selector mechanism. Number plate, engine compartment and boot illumination lights. Rheostat controlled instrument lights. Self-cancelling turn indicators with warning lights. Red warning lights on door trailing edges. Hazard flasher. Interior lights with courtesy delay. Steering column lock switches on doors and thermal illumination. Illuminated electric clock and cigar lighter. Combined twin-bladed two-speed self-parking electric windscreen wipers with anti-lift blades. Windtone and air horns with changeover switch. Electrically operated screen washers, windows and fuel door. Driver controlled electric passenger door lock. Electrically operated hood and rear quarter lights.

Body

Steel body mounted on tubular chassis giving four-seater accommodation. Sundym glass. Adjustable

interior anti-dazzle safety rear view mirror. Front Inertia reel safety belts. Front seats fitted with finely adjustable reclining hinges, incorporating quick release for access to rear seats. Pillar type adjustable headrests to both front seats with detachable cushions. Connolly hide covered seats. Locking companion box and glove box. Covered pockets in rear armrests. 12 cu. ft. (.42 m 3) luggage compartment with spring loaded self-supporting lid. Power operated fully wool lined hood with 2 snap action clamps and zip-out rear window. Hood envelope incorporating inhibiting circuit isolating hood raising mechanism. Fire extinguisher.

Instruments

Speedometer, electric impulse type tachometer, battery condition indicator, oil pressure, coolant temperature and fuel gauges. Warning lights for high beam, low fuel, handbrake, brake fluid level and pad wear, oil

pressure, fuel filler door and safety belts.

Safety belts

Inertia reel single handed lap and diagonal seat belts to front seats, with warning light.

Radio

Fully transistorised push-button radio with four speakers and balance control. Automatic electrical aerial.

Heating and ventilation

Air Conditioning: Engine driven compressor with on/off switch and variable temperature control provides cool and dehumidified air to ventilation system. Heating: 4½ Kw thermo- statically controlled unit with 2 speed booster fan, windscreen demister/defroster. High level intake. Ventilation: Four individually controllable fresh air outlets at face level delivering refrigerated or ambient temperature air.

Jacking system

Bevelift type system operating in conjunction with special lifting points.

JENSEN MOTORS LIMITED
WEST BROMWICH ENGLAND
March 1974

15M/03/74

Important

When this publication was produced the information given was correct but we reserve the right to alter details of specifications, colours or equipment without notice.

DIM	DESCRIPTION	INS.	MM
A	Overall Height	54.375	1381.1
C	... Length	184.5	4686.3
D	... Width	69	1754
E	Wheelbase	105	2667
F	Track (Front)	56.125	1425.5
G	... (Rear)	56.87	1444.5
H	Ground Clearance	5.5	139.7
J	Seat to Accelerator Pedal	34.44	863.1/176
K	Front Seat to Roof	38.5	977.9
L	Rear Seat to Roof	34.5	876.3
	Steering Wheel to Seat Clearance	6	152.5
M	... Accelerator Pedal	23.25	584.685
N	Rear Squab to Floor	21	533.4
O	Rear Seat Thigh Room	19	482.6
P	Length of Boot	34	863.6
Q	Boot Capacity	12 Cubic Feet	

JENSEN INTERCEPTOR
CONVERTIBLE

Specification of Jensen Convertible

Engine

Chrysler 90° Vee 8, O.H.V. with hydraulic tappets. Bore 4.32 in. Stroke 3.75 in. Cubic Capacity 440 cu. in. (7,212 cc) Compression ratio 8.2:1.
Crankshaft: Fully balanced. 5 main bearings. Fitted with torsional vibration damper. Lubrication system: Externally mounted rotor type pump with separate full flow filter. Fuel system: Mechanical pump. Filter in fuel line. Four-barrel carburettor with automatic thermostatically controlled choke. Flashing low fuel-level warning light operative below 3 gallons. (Imp.) 13 litres. Tank capacity 20 gallons (Imp.) 91 litres. Large capacity paper element air cleaner. Ignition: Electronic automatic centrifugal and vacuum advance. Ballast resistor for initial spark boost.
Cooling: High pressure (13 lb. sq. in.) system with pellet type thermostat. Twin thermostatically controlled electric cooling fans.

Transmission

Torqueflite Hi-Performance 3-speed automatic with torque converter. Over-riding hold controls, kickdown. Centrally mounted quadrant. Overall ratios:
1st   7.50
2nd   4.44
3rd   3.07
Reverse   6.74
Transmission oil cooler incorporated in radiator side tank. Open propeller shaft. Hypoid rear axle incorporating 'Pow'Lok' limited slip differential. Axle ratio 3.07:1

Suspension

Front: Independent coil and wishbone with telescopic type dampers. Stabiliser bar. Rear: Semi-elliptic dual rate springs with rubber button interleaved separators. Armstrong telescopic dampers, Panhard rod.

Steering

Power assisted. 15 in. diameter leather covered steering wheel with 2 in. reach adjustment. 3.4 turns lock to lock: 17.1:1 ratio. Turning circle 38 ft. steering column lock.

Wheels and tyres

Aluminium alloy cast wheels with Dunlop ER 70 VR 15 tubed tyres suitable for sustained speeds up to 110 mph without increasing pressure. Spare wheel in carrier underneath luggage compartment.

Brakes

Hydraulically operated self-adjusting Girling ventilated disc brakes on all four wheels. Separate systems for front and rear brakes with tandem master cylinder and servo assistance. Load conscious valve in rear system to prevent rear wheel lock-up. Swept area 417 sq. in. Central hand lever operates self-adjusting brakes on rear wheels. Brake pad wear indicator.

Electric equipment

12 volt 65 amp alternator with 6 silicon rectifiers. Transistorised voltage regulator. Battery 66 a/h. Four 5¾ in. Quartz halogen headlights. Side, and Dual Intensity rear lights. Reversing light operated by switch incorporated in gear selector mechanism. Number plate, engine compartment and boot illumination lights. Rheostat controlled instrument lights. Self-cancelling turn indicators with warning lights. Red warning lights on door trailing edges. Hazard flasher. Interior lights with courtesy switches on doors and thermal delay. Steering column lock illumination. Illuminated electric clock and cigar lighter. Combined twin-bladed two-speed self-parking electric windscreen wipers with anti-lift blades. Windtone and air horns with changeover switch. Electrically operated screen washers, windows and fuel door. Driver controlled electric passenger door lock. Electric demister/de-icer for rear window.

Instruments

Speedometer, electric impulse type tachometer, battery condition indicator, oil pressure, coolant temperature and fuel gauges. Warning lights for high beam, low fuel, handbrake, brake fluid level and pad wear, oil pressure, fuel filler door and safety belts.

Body

Steel body mounted on tubular chassis giving four-seater accommodation.

Sundym glass. Adjustable interior anti-dazzle safety rear view mirror. Front Inertia reel safety belts. Front seats fitted with finely adjustable reclining hinges, incorporating quick release for access to rear seats. Pillar type adjustable headrests to both front seats with detachable cushions. Connolly hide covered seats. Locking companion box and glove box. Covered pockets in rear armrests. 12 cu. ft. (.42 m 3) luggage compartment with spring loaded self-supporting lid. Fire extinguisher.

Safety belts

Inertia reel single handed lap and diagonal seat belts to front seats with warning light.

Radio

Fully transistorised push-button radio with four speakers and balance control. Automatic electrical aerial.

Heating and ventilation

Air Conditioning: Engine driven compressor with on/off switch and variable temperature control provides cool and dehumidified air to ventilation system.
Heating: 4¼ kW thermostatically controlled unit with 2-speed booster fan, windscreen demister/defroster. High level intake.
Ventilation: Throughflow system with extractor vents in rear quarter panels. Four individually controllable fresh air outlets at face level delivering refrigerated or ambient temperature air.

Jacking system

Bevelift type system operating in conjunction with special lifting points.

JENSEN INTERCEPTOR III

5ft 5in · 4ft 8in · 4ft 9¾in · 8ft 9in · 15ft 4½in · 5ft 9in · 35in · 36in · 23in–25in · 34in–44in · 3.5in · 19in

Important

When this publication was produced the information given was correct but we reserve the right to alter details of specifications, colours or equipment without notice.

JENSEN MOTORS LIMITED
WEST BROMWICH ENGLAND

March 1974

Specification of Jensen Interceptor Mk 111